THE STOLEN CHILD

THE STOLEN CHILD

JOE DUNNE

The publishers would like to thank A. P. Watt (acting on behalf of Michael B. Yeats) for permission to use lines from 'The Stolen Child' by W. B. Yeats.

First published in 2003 by Marino Books
An imprint of Mercier Press
Douglas Village, Cork
Email: books@mercierpress.ie
Website: www.mercierpress.ie

Trade enquiries to CMD Distribution
55A Spruce Avenue
Stillorgan Industrial Park
Blackrock, County Dublin
Tel: (01) 294 2560; Fax: (01) 294 2564
E-mail: cmd@columba.ie

© Joe Dunne 2003
ISBN 1 86023 153 5
10 9 8 7 6 5 4 3 2 1

A CIP record for this title is available
from the British Library

Cover design by Marino Design

Printed in Ireland by ColourBooks,
Baldoyle Industrial Estate, Dublin 13

CONTENTS

Come away, O human child!
To the waters and the wild
With a faery, hand in hand,
For the world's more full of weeping than you
        can understand.

from 'The Stolen Child' by W. B. Yeats

Dedicated with deep affection to Agnes, my close friend for sixty-five years and my dear wife for fifty.

Also dedicated to Emma, Eileen, Robert, Lynsey, Ryan, Heather, Andrew and Matthew, who live in a more enlightened and Christian Ireland, and who thankfully didn't see the Ireland that their granddad knew.

PREFACE

Modern Irish history is concerned almost solely with Ireland's political, commercial and economic developments in the decades following the emergence of the new state, so today's generation of Irish people may know little else about society in the period from, say, 1922 to 1950. They may not realise the enormous influence that religion had on the people – how it dominated their lives. Outwardly it was a very pious and Christian era; strangers from abroad would have noted at once the many signs of religious piety to be seen everywhere. Even daily conversation was flavoured with religion, God being reverently invoked at the drop of a hat.

The Church was more powerful than the state, and a militant Catholicism was everywhere evident. Churches overflowed on Sundays and holy days of obligation; novenas abounded to various saints; Corpus Christi processions were held in the public streets of many parishes, disrupting trade and traffic. Crowds flocked in their hundreds to walk in Marian processions in Mount Argus and Inchicore in Dublin. Hymns were sung and prayers recited in these processions, and altogether the emphasis was on ostentation and outward show. Annual retreats – one week for women and one week for men – were immediately followed by confessions on a large scale. Lenten fasting was observed, and it was the people, not the clergy, who policed its strict observance. The official censor had a busy time banning books, including some of the classics and some by Irish authors. Certain periodicals suffered permanent or long-time bans, and at times the censor was stung into action when the public thought he was remiss. For good measure, Radio Athlone and its successor, Radio Éireann, banned the occasional popular song from the air because it was thought sexually suggestive, or was disrespectful to the Catholic religion.

The term 'Irish Catholic' was prevalent abroad during that era, being considered a more devout and intense form of Catholicism than Roman Catholicism, as though it were a distinct religious denomination. Despite the strictness of the religious regime (which was willingly accepted by the population), the era saw many cruelties and grave injustices. The victims were the orphans of the poor, unmarried mothers and the aged poor. These suffered in their thousands (in the name of Christian charity) and the general public was not only aware of the cruelties but also colluded in them, sometimes initiating them.

Sin and scandal were seen where none existed. A woman observed entering a public house, or smoking in the street, lost her reputation. An unaccompanied man seen visiting the home of a widow scandalised the neighbourhood and was reported to the local priest or convent. Such situations resulted in children being committed to institutions until they reached the age of sixteen – in effect, a sentence of ten to twelve years in most cases. Charitable organisations also abused their positions by initiating action resulting in children being forcibly taken from their homes and 'put away'.

There were more than fifty industrial schools in the land, all of which had to be supplied with a steady intake of children, for which the state paid a small per capita grant to the religious orders who ran the schools. The more children they housed, the higher their income. Incredibly, the state permitted the law courts to be used as pawns in this process of feeding children to the hungry industrial schools – in effect, making legal the kidnapping of children. They were arraigned before the courts under false charges of convenience. Their widowed parent was not charged with failing to provide 'proper guardianship' or 'proper care and attention'; it was the children who were charged with being in need of them. Henceforth the charge appeared after their names on official records in the Departments of Justice and Education, and in the institution to which the court committed them. By this means they lost their identity as 'orphan', which may explain why so few orphans existed in an age when the country was scourged by tuberculosis, to which so many young fathers succumbed.

The final act of cruelty by the state was the inclusion of industrial schools in its penal system. This system criminalised the thousands of young boys and girls who were sent to those schools and they bore the shame and stigma for the rest of their lives. On leaving school, while they were struggling for a foothold in a strange, hostile world, often without a single relative or friend to help, they faced a heavy burden of scorn and prejudice, which they were ill-equipped to bear. Moreover, most were exploited and victimised by unscrupulous employers who looked on industrial schools as a source of cheap labour. That such extreme piety and religious observance – which was displayed before the world in those days – should exist hand in hand with such covert cruelty and injustice, and on so large a scale, was surely the ultimate hypocrisy. A militant, intense form of Catholicism was everywhere observed – and how! But true Christianity was little known, or practised.

The period from 1922 to 1950 was not a good time for children generally in Ireland. Corporal punishment was commonplace in every school in the land, and in many family homes as well. In fact, it flourished until 1982, when it was outlawed. The rod, strap or cane was the teachers' sceptre of power, the symbol of authority, and its daily use was part of the teaching culture. The teachers' unions claimed that their members acted *in loco parentis*, which gave them the rights and privileges exercised by the children's parents. Human nature being what it is, and given the cruel age that was in it, corporal punishment was often inflicted excessively, and for trivial offences. Children saw schools as places of suffering and fear, and sometimes of terror. Every hardware shop sold bamboo canes – one end crooked like a walking stick – for use on children in the family home. They were hooked in bundles to the ceiling, or high on the wall near the door to catch the eye of the passer-by, and were used by the mother; the father preferred his belt. Not all families indulged, of course. Some parents strongly disapproved of child-beating, and brought their complaints to the teacher and the Department of Education, but got nowhere. These complaints appeared regularly in the letters pages of the newspapers, but got little support from the general public, and none at all from the newspapers. The fact was that corporal punishment was not illegal; successive governments knew that it was carried out; it had the blessing of the Church and the knowledge and approval of most sections of society. When I left school I witnessed children playing on Sandymount Strand in the summer heatwaves, the weals exposed on their backs for all to see. I observed canes hanging beside the chimney breast in friends' homes, and the father's spare leather belt hanging on the door for convenience.

Some of these incidents are threaded through my story to place them in context, and in the interest of veracity. The story is about my life in two industrial schools in the 1920s and 1930s, and my struggle to adjust to a new life afterwards. But notwithstanding the mental and physical pain I endured in my more tender years, my childhood was in the main a happy one – especially that portion spent in the care of the Christian Brothers and I am glad to place that on record.

I did invite a few Old Boys to contribute their experiences too, but sadly they declined, so I was obliged to rely on my own recollections. But I understand their reluctance to speak, even after more than half a century, for it isn't easy to rid oneself of a stigma: a brand, once burnt into place, remains for life.

In common with thousands of men and women who, as children, had been cruelly committed to industrial schools, I am ashamed of my childhood background because of the public odium in which we were held. Although the schools were frequently described as reform schools and houses of correction, they were in fact orphanages, because the vast majority of the children in them were orphans. Most had lost their father, in an age when that meant financial disaster for the surviving family members, who lived on in poverty and penury. The concept of working mothers hadn't yet arrived, and most of the social welfare benefits available today were unheard of then. As they grew older, the children gradually came to realise that they had been rejected by society, but this fact was confirmed only too painfully when they left school. Then the cruel public of the day –

the grandparents or great-grandparents of present-day Irishmen and women – shunned and exploited them and treated them as young jailbirds. The shame lasted all their lives. Trades unions refused to recognise as valid the apprenticeships served by the boys in school and barred them from membership, thus exposing them to exploitation.

Those old schoolmates who still survive and who are mentioned in my story are in their seventies and eighties now, yet after all those years I have had to hide their identities under false names to protect their secret because the prejudice towards those educated in industrial schools still survives among my generation.

When I retired I thought it safe to open – by just a chink – the protective casing around my past in order to give some new acquaintances a brief glimpse of life as I had known it in my early days. That glimpse consisted of a short account of my First Holy Communion, which I was required to submit to the facilitator of the creative-writing group that I had recently joined. My account aroused the interest of the younger members, who enthusiastically asked for more. Indeed, they claimed it as a right, saying: 'To people of our generation what you described is history – not the history we read in school, but history nonetheless. It should be passed on. You haven't the right to take it with you.' And so it came about that, by writing forward and backward from my account of my First Holy Communion, I managed to put all my recollections of childhood into place. Even so, this was done merely as a therapeutic exercise in my retirement, and not with publication in mind, for I had intended to take my secret with me, as thousands have done before me. Since then I have changed my mind and have come to realise that unless people of my generation speak out, a minor though important part of history may be lost.

I was born in 1923, but my story begins in 1927, because that's as far back as my memory goes. It's a long time ago, and as I said, I was obliged to rely on my own recollections. Knowing, however, that memory can sometimes play tricks, I must allow the possibility that some episodes may have become warped by the passage of time. If that has occurred, I apologise to my few surviving companions and playmates from that distant yesterday.

JOE DUNNE
DUBLIN

1

EARLIEST RECOLLECTIONS

Several narrow streets lie between the North Strand road in Dublin and the Dublin–Belfast railway line, once known as the Great Northern. One of those narrow streets, Northbrook Avenue, forks at the end to form Northbrook Terrace, in one of whose two-storey cottages, near the railway embankment, I lived with Mammy and my sister Una.

My story opens on the first Sunday of May, 1927. I was four. The day was warm enough for the tar to melt on the road, and I was riding my tricycle round the block. After a while I tired of that and sat down to play with the tar. Mammy rushed out, excited and cross, slapped me hard on the back of the hand, carried me back inside and, with butter, began roughly cleaning my hands, scolding me all the while.

The author's mother in 1922

It wasn't my first time to mess with tar – tar and I were mutually attracted – but Mammy had never slapped me before. 'You're lucky I spotted you in time, before you got tar all over your suit, and me after putting it on specially for the procession.' She vented her anger on the stubborn stains, not realising how painful it was for me. Una – then aged five and a half – was ready to go, her black hair and eyes contrasting with her white satin dress, floral wreath and veil of fine lace. She was impatient to be off to the May procession in Inchicore, on the other side of town. I was sobbing hard now, but after a while Mammy tried to comfort me. 'There, there,' she said, 'it's all over now, everything's all right.' But I was stubborn, and wouldn't give in.

Until then, Mammy had only scolded me, usually for being awake after I was tucked in for the night. She didn't seem to understand that it was the grown-ups laughing and singing downstairs who kept me awake. Late-night 'hooleys' were frequent in our house, and the disturbance they caused the neighbours was to have dire consequences. Sometimes Mammy lifted me from my bed and carried me down to the revellers, chiding me as she went. 'Why can't you be good like Una, and go to sleep when you're told?' she would say. I still have vague memories of 'Uncle' Patrick swaying strangely in the centre of the room.

'There there,' Mammy said again, hugging me to her breast. 'Shh! Daddy's watching from heaven, and you don't want him to see you crying now, do you?'

I had no memory of Daddy, because I had been only ten months old when he died, and the thought of him in heaven, watching over me, made me stop. All through my life I would be trying to please the father I loved but had never known. An insurance agent by profession, he died of pneumonia in 1924. He was sixty-four and Mammy was thirty-three. Their marriage was the second for him, and there were no children from the first marriage. That is practically all I know about my father and – maybe because I never learned of his human imperfections – I regarded him as a sacred icon, a saint to whom I later prayed for protection and guidance.

We were ready to go to Inchicore, so away we headed to the North Strand for the electric tram, then Dublin's transport system. 'Uncle' Patrick, whose frequent visits to our house were also a source of scandal to the neighbours, held my hand. Mammy and Una preferred to be downstairs in the tram, but the two 'men' went upstairs and sat in the front, which was open to the sky. Faster and faster I urged the tram on, making wailing sounds like its own, though these gave a false impression of speed, as did the tram's lurching from side to side. 'Uncle' Patrick sat smoking his pipe and studied the racing pages of the newspaper.

He didn't like the tram, and walked everywhere except when he was with us. And didn't he love walking! It showed in his gait: body stiff, arms swinging, head erect. But for his pipe (seldom out of his mouth), he might have been a soldier on parade. He was also fond of talking; if it wasn't about horses, it was about his experiences in the Great War. The latter subject was dear to his heart, especially when he had what Mammy called 'a sup in'. Then she'd say dismissively, 'Go 'way and lose yourself; I've no time for your nonsense.'

Many years later I learned that she had been with Cumann na mBan, a kind of women's auxiliary corps during the Troubles, carrying messages and on the lookout, in the service of the old IRA. She had no time for Patrick's exploits on the side of the English.

In College Green we joined the crowd waiting for a number 21 tram for Inchicore. It was amazing to see the huge number of children converging from all directions, the girls in wreath and veil, like mini brides, the boys in white linen suits. Over the tram hung a pall of solemn-faced piety; hardly a word was spoken, as if the devotions to Our Lady had already begun.

Behind the Oblates' church was a large field where the people in their thousands walked four abreast, in a procession winding back on itself many times. It was headed by a brass and reed band, supplied by a boys' orphanage. Several rosaries were recited and hymns to Our Lady sung between the decades. A large number of women wore pale blue cloaks over street clothes, which proclaimed them 'Children of Mary'. Various sodalities, divided into confraternities (in which men and women were segregated), walked behind their respective banners, followed by the thousands who had come from outside the parish. The people finally congregated before a grotto and statue of the Virgin, to hear a sermon and Benediction. Of course I don't remember the event in great detail, being then only four years old, but I would be 'walking' again years later and, because the ceremonies never varied, it is safe to say that the above description fits the first procession I attended in 1927.

The ceremonies over, the band entertained the crowd in the clearing in front of the church. How I envied those boys in the band! As Mammy was often to remind me years later, I announced, 'When I'm big, I'm going to play in a band like that.' You'll presently see how prophetic that turned out to be.

Mammy wasn't happy living in Northbrook Terrace, judging by the way she spoke about our previous house in Fitzroy Avenue, Drumcondra – then a fashionable part of the city – where we lived after Daddy died. 'Some day, when we're on our feet again, we'll move back there,' she'd say wistfully, little knowing that the day would come when she'd see our time in Northbrook Terrace as 'the good old days' and the cottage as a palace.

I was to learn years later that it was a time of highly charged religious fervour, with packed churches, strict Lenten fasting, sodalities, confraternities, Children of Mary, annual retreats and novenas, and public Corpus Christi and Marian processions the predominant features of life in Dublin and the country at large. The Catholic Church was a mighty power in the land, and soon we would see national celebrations of the centenary of Catholic emancipation, in 1929, and the International Eucharistic Congress in 1932. Those events would leave the state awash with religious fervour, moral rectitude and prudish piety for many decades – a regime the people willingly accepted.

Presently there occurred that process of events that would have a lifelong effect on Una and me. It began with unwelcome visits from two Sisters of Charity from North William Street convent. One of them (I didn't know which) was called Sister Duggan. Mammy would look down the street and see the nuns looming in the distance, heading towards our house. She'd blanch, make the sign of the cross and say, 'Holy Mother, here comes Sister Duggan', which made us think that the nuns had only one name between them. Mammy's reaction frightened Una and me, and we'd hide till the nuns had gone. We'd see her later sobbing quietly to herself. How I hated those nuns.

My mother – then a widow for four years – was being courted by 'Uncle' Patrick, who was seen to be a frequent, unaccompanied visitor to our house. In the highly charged religious atmosphere of the day, his behaviour was a cause of scandal in the narrow-minded, prudish society. The neighbours complained to the local convent, and threw in the late-night parties for good measure. The nuns decided that the children were 'exposed to moral danger' and should, in the parlance of the day, be 'put away'. We were taken to court and sentenced to 'confinement in separate

The author aged four and a half

institutions until the age of sixteen'. Mammy was utterly help-less in the matter, her word no match against that of a holy nun – there could be but one outcome. She didn't part with us wil-lingly, and cried a lot as she tried to comfort us, though she need-ed comforting more. 'You're going on a lovely holiday,' she said to me. 'There'll be lots of little boys to play with, and you'll have a lovely time.'

Ten years would pass before I'd see Una again and be intro-duced by my mother saying, 'This is Una. Your sister. Don't you remember?'

'This can't be my sister,' I thought. 'This isn't Una.' In place of the bright, playful little girl whose image I'd carried so long, I saw an ashen-faced, gaunt, stooped sixteen-year-old girl, the signs of her ordeal plain to see. She was wearing a coarse, shape-less dress reaching below her knees (institutional black, relieved by a narrow white collar), black stockings and heavy boots. Her cruel regime in the Convent of Mercy had not allowed home visits in ten years. We were strangers. We shook hands formally, without a word. There were no tears. Society had robbed me of my bright, extrovert playmate and sister, and in her place tossed back this haggard, spiritless stranger. Mother knew of Una's experiences, which she described as 'horrendous', but when I asked about them I was told, 'It's best not to know.'

I remember the long train journey alone with my tearful Mammy (we had left Una the previous day at a convent in Booterstown), the long walk from the station of a strange town, and the tree-lined avenue that led up to a many-windowed grey building. We crunched on loose gravel to an arched door, which on Mammy's ring was opened by a girl. Immediately on enter-ing, I noticed the strange smell. I later learned that it was a com-bination of furniture and floor polish. In later years, the smell evoked the same fear and apprehension of that, the first crisis of my life, and would be forever associated with religious insti-tutions. Recapturing a sound or aroma even after many years brings memories of wherever I sensed them previously. My first smell of the convent was charged with the same forebod-

20

ing that I had sensed when Sister Duggan visited our house. As though to explain it, two nuns appeared, dressed in awe-inspiring black habits similar to that worn by Sister Duggan. After a moment's polite conversation with Mammy, the nuns pulled me from her embrace and, one on either side, half-led, half-carried me upstairs. I struggled and kicked out as hard as I could, my heart bursting with grief and fear, which abated when Mammy promised to wait. I became hysterical when the nuns began stripping me of my clothes, which had to be removed by force. I was naked and helpless. Nobody but Mammy had seen me like this. Those black figures, towering above me, terrorised me.

The year was 1928, and I have never forgotten the scene: the nuns' voices raised above my wails, their rough handling, the smell of the hot bath, and most of all my terror. I remember these things, not because I have exceptional memory, but because I have returned to them in my mind so often down the years. I was dumped into the bath and scrubbed, regardless of whether the soap stung my eyes, and afterwards I was painfully towelled, with no trace of the gentleness I was used to at bathtime. Almost hoarse from crying, I couldn't protest when being dressed in coarse grey clothes, or when my head was being shaved to the scalp by a very rough man. My worst moment came when I discovered that Mammy was gone. Gone! In utter disbelief I wailed, 'She said she'd wait for me. She promised.' I'd never see her again, of that I was sure, especially when the nuns assured me the opposite. The utter despair drenched me in icy shock. I sobbed for a long time, day and night, and was kept in the infirmary for many days.

2

St Patrick's, Kilkenny

My sentence was eleven years. I have learned that the charge shown on my admission documents to the convent read 'receiving alms'. The nun explained that, in the language of the day, that meant 'begging'. Until the Freedom of Information Act was passed recently, I was denied even this piece of information. It was a spurious charge. My father had left us provided for. Accompanied by three former schoolmates, I returned to Kilkenny recently to try yet again to ascertain the reason why we were committed as children. We were well received by the nuns, and when it was time to go, we were each handed an envelope and requested not to open it until we were on our way. One of the group, being partially deaf, didn't hear the instruction and opened his envelope at once. His reaction was so startling that we opened our own envelopes, to discover that we had all be charged with the same offence. We went into shock – so much so that the nun tried hard to ease the blow for us. She asked us to take into account how very different those days were, and how unjust. When I reached home I went upstairs to be alone. It was nearly fifty years since the last time I cried, at my mother's funeral.

I was committed to St Patrick's Boys' Industrial School, Kilkenny, seventy-five miles from my mother and home. Why so far away, when there were similar institutions in Dublin? Official policy was to place children where a vacancy existed at that moment, regardless of distance from his or her home town. This was another act of cruelty, since the high cost of travel denied a widowed parent visiting access.

I was to hear later of boys hailing from Marino who had been sent miles away, although the Artane institution was only a mile or two up the road; if they had been sent there, their widowed mothers could have visited often at little expense. In

NO.: 2409
....

	DESCRIPTION.
NAME ..... JOSEPH PATRICK DUNNE	HEIGHT ..... 3½ FEET .....
AGE ..... 5 YEARS BORN 25. 3. 1923	FIGURE ..... STOUT .....
DATE OF ADMISSION 31. 3. 1928	COMPLEXION FAIR .....
WHERE, when, and by whom Dublin 30. 3 Ordered to be detained G.P. Cussen	HAIR ..... FAIR .....
With what charge ..... RECEIVING ALMS	EYES ..... BLUE .....
UNDER WHAT SECTION OF ACT 58th	NOSE ..... SMALL .....
SENTENCE OF DETENTION 24. 3. 1939	MARKS ON PERSON AND OTHER
PREVIOUS CHARACTER	PECULARITIES .....
STATE IF "ILLEGITIMATE"	GENERAL HEALTH ..... GOOD .....
PARENTAGE:	EDUCATIONAL STATE.
NAMES OF PARENTS, or ..... FATHER DEAD	READS ..... NIL .....
STEP-PARENTS MRS DUNNE MOTHER	WRITES .....
ADDRESS ..... 28 NORTHBROOK TERRACE NORTH STRAND DUBLIN	CALCULATES .....
OCCUPATION	PREVIOUS INSTRUCTION
CHARACTER ..... GOOD VERY RESPECTABLE	AND FOR HOW LONG .....
CIRCUMSTANCES AND OTHER PARTICULARS	MENTAL CAPACITY ..... INTELLIGENT .....
.....	Particulars as to Leaving the
RELIGIOUS PERSUASION ..... ROMAN CATHOLIC	School by Licence or Discharge.

The author's personal details, noted on his admission to St Patrick's Boys' Industrial School in Kilkenny in 1928 those days, boy orphans of the poor and boys from broken homes were put into the care of nuns until the age of ten, when for a second time they were randomly assigned, this time to wherever a vacancy existed in a male-run institution.

The Sisters of Charity managed St Patrick's from a distance, content to leave daily routine and discipline to one man and about twenty girls. The girls supervised the cleaning and polishing of rooms and corridors, bathed and dressed the under sixes, and took charge of the dormitory areas at night. They had a free hand with us, and since they were products of institutions themselves, it was a matter of course that we should suffer frequent physical and verbal abuse. It was their way of life.

Our bedtime was half past six in the evening, but owing to the heat and brightness of the day, especially in summer, we often had problems going to sleep. The girl in charge patrolled the dormitories ominously. She would angrily pull down bedclothes to cane any boy found still awake ten minutes after bedtime. Before long, most of us became expert at faking sleep. Even so, I was once roused from a sound sleep in the middle of the night and severely caned by Mary Jo, who insisted that I had been talking. Of the frequent canings, the ones I remember most vividly are those I got when I had been innocent of wrongdoing. She gave me extra wallops for not naming the boy I was supposed to have been talking to. Needless to say, the real talker was afraid to own up, and small blame to him.

Mr Behan was the only man in the school, apart from a few farm labourers whom we rarely saw. Although at the time he seemed quite tall, in retrospect I'd say he was below average height. A jack of all trades, he was the electrician who maintained the electricity generator, the barber who cut our hair tight to the scalp (except for a two-inch fringe) and a general odd-job man, summoned when repairs of any kind were needed – broken locks and windows, minor carpentry and plumbing jobs. He also had charge of us during recreation periods, and when we washed, morning and evening. He imposed a state of terror, so that many trembled when he spoke.

Our ablutions were the same every morning, a solemn ritual performed in strict silence. Two bathtubs stood in the centre of the room, tap-end to tap-end, in which six naked boys washed, standing up. Each group or 'division' of ten, plus a monitor, was scheduled for a bath every nine or ten days. The rest, stripped to the waist, washed their heads, hands and faces at washbasins lining three sides of the room.

Mr Behan shouted orders army style, so that heads, faces, necks and ears were soaped, rinsed and dried at the same time. On the order 'turn off and wring', we turned off the taps, and with our hands brushed the water from our heads and faces, then waited for the command to dry ourselves. On another command, we about-turned to face the bathers, who had been washing independently. Each of them stepped from the bath in turn and, with arms extended, rotated slowly for Mr Behan's inspection. If Mr Behan wasn't satisfied, the boy was beaten on the body with a strap. More often than not, a bruise sustained the previous day in the normal course of play – or from a previous beating – was the cause of the trouble, being mistaken for a dirty mark.

We called this punishment a 'flogging', as distinct from a 'biffing', which we got on the palms of the hands. Once, the sight of a naked Eddie Staunton being flogged after his bath was too much for a few of the spectators, and we cried in sympathy.

'Who's that snivelling over there?' Mr Behan snapped. There was no reply. Singling me out, he pulled me by the ear into the centre of the room and demanded to know why I was crying: 'I asked you a question. What are you crying for?' But I could not think of an answer, so I got a flogging similar to Staunton's. Delivered with full force, anywhere and everywhere on the body, each stroke was accompanied by one word of a phrase he would repeat again and again: 'I'll – give – you – a – reason – to – cry!'

A boy was called a sissy or a baby if he bawled during a beating, so by keeping my tears bottled up as long as I could, I 'acted the man'. Instinctively I placed a hand to the last place to get a wallop, when I could reach it, which invited a blow elsewhere, so that hardly any part escaped. My thighs, back, buttocks, arms and legs smarted painfully long after the beating was over. For some time after this incident I woke during the night in a sweat, and I cried beneath the bedclothes for my mammy to come and take me back home. I thought of my daddy in heaven, and wondered why he allowed these things happen.

Of the hundred fellow inmates in St Patrick's, Staunton is one of the few I still remember from those outside my small circle of mates or chums. We were to meet again in our next school, and when I reminded him of the flogging he had got on that occasion, his off-hand attitude surprised me.

'Oh, that?' he said with a shrug. 'It wasn't as bad as I let on. Ye see, Behan loved to see ye bawlin' and howlin' in agony. So I played up. The quiet fellas like yerself got it until ye howled, if it was to take all day, so ye only made it harder on yerselves in the end.' I sensed bravado in his words, for he was a mature age then – thirteen, I think – and could afford to act the 'big fella' and let on he hadn't felt a thing. Yet many years later, when I was discussing our convent days with James White, one of the few old boys willing to do so, I remembered Staunton's words again, and thought maybe he was right – maybe he hadn't felt the pain as much as I had. For James also dismissed as trivial our punishments at the hands of Mr Behan, and was surprised to hear how they affected me, and how unhappy I had been in Kilkenny. It occurred to me that children may have varying degrees of physical and emotional tolerance, and may be affected differently by the same experiences.

The 'machine room' housed a large generator for the institution's electricity supply, and Mr Behan had sole charge. I was once sent to him with a message. The noise and the heavy oily smells made it a forbidding, frightening place for a timid eight-year-old, so I had no wish to stay longer than necessary. Having delivered my message I turned to go and was called back, expecting to be biffed (there didn't have to be a reason).

'Come here to me, and stand right there,' Mr Behan said, roughly pushing me in front of one of the machines. 'Now, wet your finger in your mouth and put it on that knob.' By instinct, I refused. The more I resisted, the more he pushed and pulled me, and clipped my ears, till I became so frightened that I wet the floor. He pulled my ears again and bellowed at me to do as I was told. When finally I obeyed I got an electric shock that flung me hard against the wall, leaving me sitting on the stone floor, gasping for breath. He roared laughing.

I was sent to fetch him again a few days later, and this time Mr Butler, one of the farm labourers happened to be there. 'Watch,' Mr Behan said to him, 'this is very funny.' He ordered me to touch the machine as before, but I backed away. No amount of bullying could force me to do it again. I was slapped on the face and pulled by the ears, but the electric shock held more terrors. Mr Butler returned to the farm, not wishing to see any more, which only made things worse. Mr Behan flogged me cruelly with his belt for 'embarrassing me in front of my friend'. Luckily I wasn't sent there again.

James White told me years later that he too remembered the electric shock, but he dismissed it as 'nothing'. Of course, he had not wet the floor he said, laughing, and went on to explain that a wet floor increases an electric shock, since it is a better conductor than a dry one. Whether it is true that genetic differences cause children to be affected in different ways by similar experiences I don't know, but I do believe that painful experiences go deeper in delicate children and last longer. Such children tend to harbour hurts. They brood on them with hatred for their tormentors. What the healthy child suffers only momentarily and shrugs aside as nothing, the ailing one nurtures long afterwards and, with bitterness, relives the experience when something stirs the memory.

3

The Infirmary

During my years in Kilkenny, I seemed to get every illness to which children are prone: measles, German measles, ringworm, sties and boils – especially boils – and I spent a lot of time in the infirmary. I was pining for home, and the nuns' best efforts failed to help me adjust to life in an institution. The infirmary, containing a dozen beds, was always overheated by a roaring fire, kept going all the time in winter and at night in summer. Above the heavy mantelpiece hung a large monochrome picture of St Philomena gazing at the sky in pious rapture.

Holy pictures were a big feature of my convent home. They hung every four or five yards in corridors, classrooms, in the three dormitories and in the infirmary. Those in colour emphasised the wounds or sufferings of their subjects. The dominant one in each area created the atmosphere there, and I liked or disliked the room accordingly. Some pictures were of a saint in a solemn attitude of prayer, with a trancelike expression on their upturned face, illuminated by a beam of light shafting down from the sky or through a church window. Others were of holy men, usually dark and bearded, who frowned sternly, their eyes seeming to follow my every move. Far from adorning the place, the holy pictures were intimidating and depressing. If they were intended to excite us to prayer and piety, they failed. Mostly they frightened me, and some near my bed gave me nightmares.

In certain places it wasn't a picture but a large statue that dominated the room from a wooden plinth, usually opposite the door, so it was the first thing one saw. Having defeated the challenge of several pictures, and having clinched its claim by giving its name to the room, the statue looked down its nose on the popes and saints who decorated the walls. 'St Anthony's parlour', 'Our Lady's parlour' and 'the Sacred Heart room' were examples of this.

But the infirmary was different, in spite of its share of holy pictures. The strong chemical and disinfectant smells, the heat (oh, the heat) and thirst, the fear of pain – these made me hate the place. I remember one miserable Christmas lying on my stomach, suffering from eighteen boils on my back and arms. Since they didn't mature at the same rate, the pain extended over several weeks, as each day a few at a time were squeezed clean of pus between the fingers of a not very gentle nun. I lay in bed, looking down on the train and tracks Mammy had sent me for Christmas, tantalisingly out of reach on the floor, each carriage in its own cardboard compartment. My pleas to be allowed to handle even one item were denied, until finally I was warned that the box would be taken away if I asked again.

Heat was a common factor in the treatment of all illness, and in order to maintain a high temperature in the room, the girl who assisted the nun frequently refuelled the fire. We sweated in bed, so tightly tucked in that we couldn't move. The girl or the nun made sure that we didn't place even an arm outside the bed-clothes, and many a rough awakening I got when it was discovered that I'd thrown the clothes off in my sleep.

Whatever pain our illness might bring was nothing compared to the pangs of thirst, especially at night. My pleas for a drink were answered by the night girl with a cup of hot milk, but it was always curdled, putrid and undrinkable – no wonder, since it had stood all day beside the fire in an enamel jug. I begged and pleaded for a cold drink instead, only to hear, 'I won't say no again. That's all there is to drink, I tell you. If you were real thirsty, you'd drink it. Now don't dare call me again for no reason.' How I dreaded the night, twisting and turning, waiting for the morning and its welcome tea or cocoa. A drink of water would have been even more welcome. Those are my enduring memories of the infirmary.

Occasionally we patients were visited by a lady fondly known as the 'apple woman'. Tall and beautifully dressed, she was probably a patron of the school, for the nuns unashamedly lavished attention on her whenever she came. She gave me a glass marble one day, with beautiful colours inside, and I can't describe the heights to which my joy soared, even though I was confined to bed and couldn't play with it. It was amazing the pleasure we got from owning something, even a polish-box lid, or the wheel of a broken toy. Such things were thrown out with the rubbish anywhere else, but here they were prized as play-things, and when after a while we tired of them, we swapped them for something else. Swapping was an ongoing business, and an unwritten code was observed, forbidding older boys from swapping with juniors. When a lapse occurred, an older brother or pal had the swap rescinded. Serrated cogs from a mechanical toy, now serving as a spinning top spun with the fingers, were bartered for a 'busted' rubber ball, or a tin motor car without wheels. And many a swap collapsed because one party had been a previous owner way back, and you'd hear, 'No thanks – sure, didn't I own that yoke before.' Your salesman-ship was tested when you were asked what use your 'yoke' could be put to, and it was up to you to give a convincing demonstra-tion.

But a big glass marble! Here was an original, which no boy had owned before. I foresaw that I'd be the envy of everyone for a long time to come, with many tempting swap offers. But first I would get the utmost enjoyment from it when I was better. Alas! I was to suffer the pain and disappointment of seeing it confiscated when the time came for me to leave the infirmary. In spite of my tears the nun buried it in the folds of her habit with tight-lipped finality.

'It's only for sick boys,' she said. 'It was given in the infirm-ary and it belongs here.' Grimly I determined to appeal to the apple woman when next she came, but my nerve failed.

We went for walks on Sundays along the Kells road, and I can still see the profusion of wild primroses under the hedge-rows, and the mayflower, and in autumn the blackberries. In awed silence we passed what we believed was a fairy fort, just visible through the hedge, near the crossroads. Within our reach grew a gnarled and twisted crab-apple tree, which we didn't dare touch because it belonged to the 'Little People'. After an hour or less (it was hard to gauge time), we halted for a break before turning for home. A boy with keen sight spied a tiny speck in the blue sky and shouted 'Skylark!', and we all saw it then, far above our heads. It filled the whole atmosphere about us with its song. I was amazed. A hush fell over us, all wondering how such powerful music could come from so tiny a bird. The Angelus bell ringing in distant Foulkestown provided reverent accompaniment. It is the only time I ever heard the song of a skylark. Presently, I climbed on a gate and looked below on a huge field of green corn, the breeze causing ripples like waves on a choppy lake. I relive that day in all its wonder whenever I read 'A Green Cornfield' by Christina Rossetti. She describes the scene so faithfully:

> The cornfield stretched a tender green
> To right and left beside my walks;
> I knew he had a nest unseen
> Somewhere among the million stalks:
>
> And as I paused to hear his song
> While swift the sunny moments slid,
> Perhaps his mate sat listening long
> And listened longer than I did.

Every autumn thousands of birds – the larger ones in V-formation, the smaller ones in shimmering clouds – flew directly over our school on their way to warmer climes. Autumn was also the season when the apple woman pulled up alongside us in her motor car when we were out walking. It had a canvas top, folded back if the day was warm, and because cars were very high by the standards of today, there was a running-board on each side to help her climb in. There was also a brass horn which her driver blew by squeezing a rubber bulb when we came into view. Motor cars were a rare sight in the country in the early 1930s, and each one got a hearty wave and a cheer when passing us.

In the apple season we walked with one eye over our shoulder, ears cocked for the apple woman's motor horn. From a large flour bag she distributed sweet apples to us on the roadside. We ate them ravenously, caring little about the telling off we were sure to get from Sister Bega later for not eating our dinner. Mrs Kearney, or perhaps Carney, was her name. She had a large farm in the neighbourhood, and I have often wondered since if she had had any notion of the tremendous happiness she gave us, or if she knew how much we appreciated her kindness, particularly as kindness was for us a rare experience.

The Kells road had yet to get its first ever surface of tarmacadam, and we returned to the convent completely coated in fine chalky dust raked up by our feet. Why we went on those walks I'll never know; it surely wasn't for fresh air, because the powdery dust got everywhere: into our eyes, our clothes, our hair – and presumably our lungs as well.

Thirst was an unpleasant feature of summer, not only for patients in the infirmary. Through the railings, with tear-stained envy, we watched the farm horses drink their fill from a trough in the field that lay in front of our play enclosure, and many of us resorted to drinking water that we flushed into our hands in the toilet bowls, there being no drinking water laid on in the recreation yard where a lot of our time was spent. Occasionally we lined up to receive a single leaf of lettuce, distributed from a basin by one of the girls, and it was not unusual for the lettuce to harbour a few slugs, which we ate too – why else were we given them? When the lettuce had been consumed, we fought for a share of the water remaining in the basin, but most of it was lost in the jostling.

Summer was also the season when our mattresses were cut open in the recreation yard, and we were put to work teasing out the horsehair stuffing between our fingers. Because of the large number of mattresses involved, the operation took several days. It was an extremely dusty job: the blinding, choking, smelly dust raised in the process by nearly a hundred boys is best left to the imagination. Afterwards we stuffed the hair back into the casings, which the girls sewed up again, leaving the mattresses plumper and softer than before.

Winter, on the other hand, brought its own pain. There was no heating in the recreation hall, and when the weather was coldest Mr Behan ordered us out to the recreation yard. We had to run for an hour in the frost and snow around a gazebo in the centre of the yard, and any boy slowing down got a blow on the back with the stick. We returned to the hall in abject misery, all of us in tears, much colder than before.

We were subject to Mr Behan's whistle, and had to respond promptly as a single unit. He decided when it was time to break and go to the toilet, as apparently we were all supposed to want to go at the same time, and he didn't take kindly to any boy who wanted to go outside his chosen times. Once, when I sought permission to 'go to the yard', as we called it, he refused, saying that it was only ten minutes since the last break. But I pleaded so much that he finally agreed, saying, 'All right, but I'm coming along to see that you do need to go.' As he stood menacingly beside me at the urinal, my fear of him mounted and mounted, while the pressure on my bladder – almost at bursting point a few moments before – receded rapidly, then vanished. I prayed for even a trickle to show, but it was impossible as long as Mr Behan was looking. I was 'skull-hauled' by the ear back to the hall, the boys sitting mutely on the benches. Then he announced that he was going to make an example of me, which he did by giving me a severe 'biffing'. Normally, for a 'biffing' you stood with hand outstretched, palm upwards. But this time he caught me firmly by the wrist with one hand, and with the stick in his other beat me mercilessly, then did the same on my other hand. Meanwhile, the floodgates opened, and I wet myself uncontrollably. I'll never forget the shame. I was made mop up the floor, to the jeering of some of the boys.

I was later found to have a kidney infection, which meant another spell in the infirmary.

4

The Nuns

The nuns played only a peripheral role in the running of the institution, and seemed blissfully unaware of the harshness of the regime. A few 'worker nuns', as I called them, were distinguished by the white habit they wore instead of black. These oversaw the large Magdalen-type laundry, the kitchen and the boys' workshop. Most of the nuns wore black and had little to do with the boys. They appeared among us only on periodic 'visits'. One such was Sister Victor, who visited the classrooms occasionally – before Easter, for instance – and spoke at length about Christ's Passion. Like all the nuns, she was friendly when met with on her own, but when with other nuns, or when addressing the class, she was remote, distant and supercilious.

For the seven weeks of Lent, all the statues and holy pictures were covered with purple drapes. They would not be exposed again until midday on Easter Saturday, when Lent was officially over. Lent was a solemn period; no hymns were sung, no bells were rung – Sundays and holy days excepted. Sister Victor's Lenten talks were fascinating. Her graphic account of the first Holy Thursday and her description of the Last Supper in the upper room evoked images which come to mind today when I read the Gospels. In all the years since, the images have remained the same.

She also came before Christmas, and so vivid was her story of Bethlehem that we imagined ourselves on the hillside with the shepherds while the angels sang *Gloria in Excelsis Deo*, our faces turned up to the ceiling, expecting to see the heavenly choirs. A tremendous rapport developed between Sister Victor and us. Some boys offered her their letters from home, and didn't mind when she read them out for all to hear. 'You've got a new baby brother, Peter, isn't that lovely?' or, 'Your mammy's coming to see you at Easter, Tony.'

When a nun came to the dormitories on inspection, it was almost a ceremonial occasion. We stood in respectful silence until the visit was over, the girl in charge remaining close by in case questions were asked. The rarity of inspections was what made them special, gave them an air of importance or ritual. Everywhere was scrutinised. The nun ran a finger along the wainscot looking for traces of dust (with all nuns, it seemed, dust was an obsession). She stooped to examine the underside of the iron beds, and admonished the girl in charge if she saw any 'bunting' – part of the bedclothes hanging through the diamond shapes of the bedsprings. Unfortunately for us, the reprimand was later passed on by the girl to the bed's owner, supported by smacks of the cane.

In those days only women from well-to-do families were admitted to most orders of nuns, and being considered 'Brides of Christ', it was said that they brought handsome dowries with them. Regarded as the crème de la crème among ladies, they were treated accordingly. Nuns lived on a different planet from the rest of mankind, and on the rare occasion when their lives and ours converged, their austere, superior bearing forbade closer contact. They seemed very conscious of their lofty state, and everyone treated them like royalty. We were not allowed to speak unless spoken to, and a nun rarely spoke to us directly, except when she 'addressed' us in a group, as in the classroom. A boy felt privileged to be spoken to on his own, and it was usually a friendly encounter. It happened to me occasionally when I was about my work cleaning the chapel, for we all had tasks to keep us occupied – 'the devil finds work for idle hands'.

Reverend Mother was so important that she was seldom even referred to, and then only in tones of reverence and awe. When she wasn't absent 'on business' or on visits to another convent, I'd see her heading the solemn procession of nuns from convent to chapel for devotions a couple of times a day. She led the prayers, after which the community sang hymns. Hidden in the organ gallery, I listened secretly, eavesdropping, I felt, on a choir of angels.

The author (aged eight) when he was serving as an altar boy in Kilkenny

In pre-Vatican II years, Sisters of Charity were garbed from head to foot in a voluminous black habit, folded back up from just above the floor and secured at the waist with black pins. The front of the veil lay flat above the forehead, as though shading the eyes, and the rest fell over the shoulders, ending in a point well down the back. The only part of a nun not covered by her habit was her face, which looked out through a starched wimple. Not even a wisp of hair showed. Her hands were rarely seen, each thrust into the opposite cuff. A nun seldom hurried, but when she did you might glimpse a shoe, flat and rubber-heeled. Normally she glided, fixed of purpose, across highly polished floors as though on well-oiled castors.

Before setting off in silent procession to devotions, each nun unpinned part of her habit and let it sweep the floor behind like a bride's train. This practice, and the wearing of a wedding ring, was probably designed to remind her that she was a

'Bride of Christ'. The sound of over twenty nuns walking in procession was eerie and awe-inspiring. It grew in a slow crescendo, and faded again as the nuns passed in double file, a gap of several yards behind each couple to allow space for their trains.

Sister Victor played the organ on Sundays and holy days, and trained the chapel choir. The organ wasn't an electric one, but operated by wind pressure pumped into it with a large bellows. When I was in the senior class, I was given the job of operating the bellows. It required every ounce of my weight and strength to press down the heavy lever that protruded from the organ's side and to pull it back up again, a procedure that had to be repeated for the duration of every hymn. The effort being too much for me one day, I fainted from exhaustion. Sister Victor was much concerned on my behalf, and I saw her motherly side for the first time. It removed the barrier between us. Thereafter, whenever we met she had a few sweets for me and the friendliest of smiles. The smile was like a rope thrown to a drowning person, and I'll always remember it.

Once she paid an unexpected visit to my classroom while we were at our singing lesson. She got excited on discovering that I had what she described to everyone afterwards as 'a beautiful singing voice'. I became a member of the chapel choir and was often warmly complimented for my solo singing. Singing in the choir was a real joy, and for that reason Sister Victor holds a special place in my memory. She also taught me some songs which I performed for the bishop and other important visitors. She'd accompany me on the piano and, to help me get over my nerves, would smile and bow encouragingly. 'Goodbye Ol' Ship of Mine' and 'The Old-fashioned House' were my party pieces for years afterwards. Sister Germaine too was a music-loving nun, pleasant and jolly, and very kind. From her I also learned many songs for her musical revues.

All boys over the age of about eight had work of some kind to do. Under Sister Bertha's instruction, they worked in the workshop, sewing buttons on our clothes and doing minor shoe repairs. Mr Cass, the shoemaker, attended to the major repairs. Where nowadays would you see eight- to ten-year-old children manipulating an awl and 'wax-end', their tongues peeping from the side of their mouths, sewing leather patches on their play-mates' boots? They loved the work, and had a special affection for Sister Bertha, probably because the work brought them close together. My allotted work was not in the workshop but in the chapel and corridors, polishing the wooden floors and dusting the chapel furniture under the supervision of a girl named Kath-leen. Even today, after more than half a century, the smell of wood polish never fails to evoke unhappy memories of seemingly countless hours spent pushing and pulling a heavy polishing block.

Kathleen, who was about thirty, I suppose, was short in stature, short-sighted and short-tempered. She nagged and harassed me without end; nothing pleased her. Although she wore thick spectacles, she claimed she could see specks of dust in unlikely places like the inner recesses of the ornate wrought-iron altar rails. She'd cuff me painfully on the head, saying, 'Get right into those crevices – I keep telling you.' Yet if I took extra care and cleaned some area a second time to be quite certain it would pass inspection, she would cuff me for being too slow. I also swept the stone paths between the flower beds outside the chapel. This was a pleasant task, especially since Kathleen ap-parently thought that the garden was outside her bailiwick and I was left to myself. I have happy memories of the flower gar-den, and of the birds I fed daily on crusts of bread. Some boys didn't like their crusts and were glad to give them to me for the birds. But most of my work was indoors in the chapel, under Kathleen's critical eye. It was heavy work and wearisome, and I was so miserable one day that I knelt down and sobbed my heart out. (She must have been temporarily elsewhere, or I wouldn't have dared take a break.) The seat I chose to kneel at was sacred to me, for it was on this spot that my mother had briefly knelt to pray when on her previous visit.

All through my stay in Kilkenny I suffered recurring waves

of homesickness, but the longing for my mother was for some reason stronger at that moment. Seeing her only once a year, on Visiting Day, blurred her image and she became remote and mystical. At a time of depression such as this, I prayed to her as I would to the saints. The manner in which I was wrenched from her arms when I first came to the convent had caused a ripple effect through the course of my stay, at its worst when I fell foul of some member of staff and during nights of troubled steep. I looked for a kind adult face among the girls, but there was none – not since the day, years before, when Miss Ahern, my teacher in infants' class, left to be married. She used to slip me a slice of bread and sugar (a luxury) and say, 'Don't let anyone see you. Now, give me a big hug before you go.' That was what I missed most during my tender years in Kilkenny: a human touch. Instead, physical punishment and the fear of it loomed constantly before me, even over-shadowing playtime. It affected my appetite and health, and my school-learning too, because of absences when I was in the infirmary. I was a frequent victim of Miss O'Reilly's stick in class. The wretched circle was complete, and my cup of misery full.

As I knelt in tears that day in the chapel, silently pouring out my miseries to my invisible mother, it happened that I was observed by Sister Ursula, who was dressing the altar with clean linen. She misinterpreted what she saw and told her community that she had never seen a boy so devout at his prayers. From then on, she harped on the idea of my becoming a priest when I grew up. I was an altar boy already, and served Sunday Mass only twice a month or so, but from now on I would be serving the nuns' Mass at seven every morning.

The girl who woke me at half past six returned to bed behind her curtain, leaving me all alone. I was terrified in the dimly lit corridors on the way to the chapel. The eyes in the holy pictures followed me menacingly, and as my pace quickened, so did my heartbeat. To ward off whatever threatened and to underpin my courage, I marched as noisily as I could along the polished floor, and even made a feeble attempt at whistling.

During Mass I said the Latin responses to Father Byrne in a rapid, sing-song monotone, not understanding the meaning of a single word that either he or I was saying throughout the long service. Had I understood the meaning itself, I was not old enough to appreciate the irony in my response: '*Et in troibo ad altare Dei, ad Deum qui laetificat juventutem meam*' ('And I will go unto the altar of God, unto God who giveth joy to my youth'). I had learned the Latin responses parrot-fashion from a senior altar boy, and in due course, in exactly the same way, I would pass them on to a junior boy coming after me.

While the priest read the long Epistle in Latin with both hands raised to shoulder level and his back towards me and the congregation of nuns, each nun in her own *prie-dieu*, I had to watch for either a slight gesture of his left hand or a nod of his head, this being the signal that he was coming to the end of the readings. At that point I should mount the steps of the altar and be at his side to transfer the missal to the Gospel side. In the dim light of the chapel, at seven in the morning, I wasn't always alert enough to see the signal. I would sometimes miss it through concentrating on his hand the very morning that he decided to signal with his head. This infuriated the priest, and he would turn round towards me with an impatient snap of his fingers that echoed round the chapel. This exaggerated the gravity of my lapse. My mouth dried up and I was almost sick from worry as we approached that stage of the Mass – which is hardly surprising in view of the climate of fear in which I lived all the time. Despite these lapses, however, I was selected to serve Mass for Doctor Collier, Bishop of Ossory, whenever he visited the convent (which was about twice a year) and I was trained to act as waiter at the special lunch for him and the nuns.

Another of my special tasks was to guide Sister Coman to her pew in the chapel for nuns' devotions, and back again to the convent afterwards. Despite being totally blind, and very stout, Sister Coman walked fast and with reckless disregard for where she was going. It was my task to make sure she didn't tread on the train of the nun in front of her in the procession. I was not always successful in this, and the victim gave me a roasting for *my* clumsiness. But I was helpless and could only guide the nun; I couldn't slow her down. In the end I was told to wait until all the others had gone ahead. We must have looked a comical pair, I holding her soft, podgy hand, she saying, 'Our own little procession', as she plodded heavily along, the floorboards complaining under her weight. I think she sometimes lost her bearings and forgot where she was, as for instance when she told me that when polishing my shoes I should be sure to put plenty of polish between the upper and the sole 'to keep the weather from getting in' – advice which, though sound in its own way, I suppose, is hardly appropriate when walking up the aisle of a convent chapel.

5

DENTISTS AND TREATS

Joe White was my closest pal all through my school years. When the Second World War came, he joined the RAF and afterwards settled in England for good. Joe's older brother James joined the British merchant navy, and for the duration of the war he sailed in the North Atlantic convoys. As small boys, neither had been affected in the slightest by the rigours of the convent years, while I, in contrast, had suffered awful pangs of loneliness and homesickness. They took everything on the chin, for which I admired them. Their indomitable spirit was inherited from their father, who had fought in the Troubles, and later as a Free State army lieutenant in the Civil War. He disappeared in 1927, as a result of the bitterness that continued to prevail after that conflict. Woven through my friendship with Joe was a strong though friendly rivalry. As I said, I envied him, and regarded him as an elder brother. Our standards in the classroom were fairly level, but I privately acknowledged him as 'the better man' all round. Keeping pace with him was a struggle for me.

I remember, at the age of six or so, him telling me about hell, the kind of people who went there, and what happened to them. I was appalled, and we argued about it all the time. I wouldn't believe him, chiefly because God, I insisted, was too good to allow that sort of thing to happen, and besides, it was too far-fetched anyway. Joe was backed up by some older boys, and I ridiculed them as well. The matter was finally settled when I plucked up courage and asked Sister Victor. I was devastated by her answer, for, against increasing odds, I had been vigorously defending the goodness of God for a whole week, and all for nothing. My faith suffered a severe jolt, and I fell out with Joe, ostensibly because he made me look a fool in front of everybody, but really because he was right. That was one thing about him – he was always right, and his 'I told you so' came a little too often for my liking.

Another thing I didn't like: he was always first with the news, as for instance when, a few years later, he brought the news about two dentists coming to the school.

'Dentists? What are dentists?' I asked.

'They're comin' to have a look at our teeth.'

'What would they want to see our teeth for?'

'To see if they're clean, I suppose,' he said. 'Mary Jo told me they want to clean them for us if they're not.' Since we never cleaned our teeth, it seemed reasonable that someone should do it for us. And he was right about the dentists, for didn't they appear the next day. 'See, I told you so,' he said with a superior air, adding for good measure, 'There's a fat one and a skinny one.'

One at a time we were brought to see the dentists, and while waiting for our name to be called, we wondered why no boys were coming back to us. We were dying to hear how they got on, but chiefly we wanted to settle a bet as to which dentist was 'the best'. I was escorted by one of the girls to the anteroom of the infirmary and ushered in to two white-coated strangers, a fat one and a skinny one, as Joe had said. I was put sitting in a strange chair and told to 'open wide'. The skinny dentist looked at my teeth, talking to me all the while, asking my name and age and what class I was in, all of which I answered as well as the little mirror he held in my mouth allowed.

Suddenly the chair was tilted back and the fat dentist pinned my arms. The other gripped one of my teeth in a pincers and, after giving it a few agonising twists, pulled it right out. I could not believe the pain. Never had I felt anything like it before. It was worse than a dozen boils being squeezed at the same time. I roared and bawled, twisted and squirmed and struggled as hard as I could, but there was no escape. Seven more teeth were extracted in this way, without anaesthetic, the fat man pinning my body to the chair, a girl holding on to my feet. The dentists' anaesthetic known as 'Twilight Sleep' was not known at the time – or if it was, they didn't bother with it. After each extraction I was told to spit into a small dish, where the sight of so much blood sent fresh shivers of fear through me. By the time they were finished I was in severe shock, dazed and shivering uncontrollably with the cold.

All through my agony Sister Vianny roundly scolded me for struggling so hard and for being 'such a baby', but believe me, the pain truly was unbearable. Afterwards I realised why none of the boys had been allowed to return, to mingle with those still waiting. Had any inkling of what lay ahead seeped back to the waiting boys, the resulting panic and hysteria could not have been controlled. In the infirmary, the worst-affected boys were fed on 'goodie' for a week – bread and warm milk sprinkled with sugar. I had often seen it made for one or two infants, and had licked my lips longingly for a taste. Now I couldn't believe my disappointment at the awfulness of it.

It wasn't all sorrow, pain and sickness in Kilkenny Convent. There were some happy moments too. There were the presents my mother sent me twice a year – sweets for my birthday in March contained in a John Players' tin tobacco box, with its bearded sailor trade mark on the lid. That was exciting, even though the whole lot had to be handed up to the nun, box and all. She doled the sweets back to me, a few every other day. I would have willingly exchanged the sweets for the box, to play with and barter for something else later on, but I never got it back.

There was also my mother's Christmas present, the same every year: a clockwork train and tracks. It hardly ever survived longer than a week because so many boys shared it, since they had no relatives to send them presents. Every November the boys who had a mammy or a daddy wrote their Christmas letter home, saying what they wanted for Christmas. It was written out for us on the blackboard by a nun, with a space left for each boy to write in which toy he wanted. We copied it laboriously into a jotter with much licking of pencils and rubbing out. I never failed to ask for trains and tracks, because I had lived near the railway and they reminded me of home. My mother's letter was read to me by Sister Victor or Sister Germaine. The other boys thronged around to listen, as envious of me as I was of them when I heard their letters read out. Thereafter, I tried to read the letter myself again and again, until it came apart from being folded and unfolded so often. Even then I slept with the remnants under my pillow, sacred relics of my mother.

My mother married 'Uncle' Patrick within a year of my coming to Kilkenny, and her letter was read aloud for me by a nun. I wouldn't accept it, and resented the term 'new daddy', because nobody in the world could take my daddy's place. 'Uncle' Patrick accompanied Mammy once a year on Visiting Day, the August Bank Holiday, at the cheap train 'excursion' rate of six shillings. My mother couldn't afford to come more often, and it was many years before I learned what sacrifices she made, and how hard she scrimped and saved for the train fare and for the goodies she brought me.

Visiting was also allowed on the Easter and Whit Bank Holidays, but as I hadn't noticed that she came only in August, I cried with bitter disappointment on those days. We were assigned Saint Anthony's parlour to ourselves, the other boys' 'people' (and there were many) having to share a large common room. Also for some reason my 'people' were the only ones given a conducted tour of the school. My desk in the classroom, my place in the refectory, and my bed in the dormitory were pointed out by one of the nuns, as if they were special.

Hanging on the wall near my bed was a picture showing Saint Rock (or Roque) staring up to heaven while a ferocious-looking wolf or large dog licked running sores on the saint's legs. My mother was appalled, and asked if I was frightened by it. I said I was. The nun promptly removed it and I was glad, for my eyes used fix on that picture while waiting for sleep to come, all sorts of fantasies tormenting me. The special status given my mother and stepfather puzzled me and my pals. It was also strange that, in my final two years, I alone was allowed home for a week each summer. I heard long afterwards from an old aunt that some of the money willed by my father had been assigned, presumably by the courts, towards my school expenses, but I had no means to find out if it were true, nor did I ever learn more about a will.

Occasionally 'the girls' staged a concert in the large classroom, and Sister Germaine produced shows by the boys too. Although rehearsing was hard work, we got a great kick out of them, because the nuns were in light-hearted mood, having shed their severe manner and come down to earth. On one occasion, in 1930 or 1931, Jimmy O'Dea, the famous Irish comedian, brought his summer show to the convent . It was unforgettable, and we experienced a taste of heaven. I can still recall the popular songs of the day, 'My Old Kentucky Home' and 'When it's Springtime in the Rockies'. I will always retain a mental tableau of the dapper little dark-haired man (as Jimmy was then), backed by the entire company, their hands high in the air, singing the final chorus:

Cheerio, let it go,
Every maid and every chappie
Don't be peevish, don't be snappy,
Make your mind up to be happy.
C–h–e–e–r–i–o!

The message, I felt, was meant for me personally. When I grew up I never missed an O'Dea pantomime or summer show in Dublin's Gaiety Theatre. How often had I felt the urge to call to the stage door after the show to remind Mr O'Dea of that exciting event of my childhood, and to let him know the tremendous joy and uplift he had given me when I so badly needed it. But years of not speaking unless spoken to have left a deep stamp upon my character, which doubtless explains why, to my great regret, I never took that step.

Breakfast was always bread and margarine with tea. The evening meal was the same, except that we sometimes had cocoa instead of tea. The bread was a couple of inches thick and had been smeared with margarine by the kitchen staff. It was already in place when we filed into the refectory.

Dinner most days was stew eaten with a spoon, knives and forks being unknown. On Fridays and days of abstinence (when meat was forbidden by the Church under pain of mortal sin), we had stirabout or maybe a boiled egg, which sat in a round hole that had been pressed out of the bread with an eggcup. Rice, with a spoonful of stewed rhubarb in the middle in summer, was our Sunday dinner.

The tables in the refectory were covered by oil-cloth table-cloths, and when a boy accidentally spilt anything he had to lap it up like a cat – that is, until the day when Sister Bertha, happening to come in unexpectedly, saw a boy in the process of licking up his spillage. She was quite angry with Mary Jo, the girl in charge, who, to my amazement, denied all knowledge of what was going on. Thankfully, we didn't have to do it any more from then on.

Christmas was largely a non-event, despite visible signs three weeks before its arrival. A sprig of holly or ivy draped over the top of every holy picture passed for festive decoration, and a few plum puddings hanging in cloths from the ceiling at one end of the refectory failed to excite us, since we knew they were for the convent and staff. Christmas Day itself was distinguished as the only weekday on which, after our main meal of stew, we had dessert of rice and jam. Then we filed into the large classroom, where stood a tall glass cabinet displaying small toys: wooden spinning tops, lead soldiers, clockwork motor cars, mouth organs and bugles. We approached in single file, to be ceremonially presented with a toy, the proceedings presided over by the Reverend Mother herself. That and Easter were the occasions when she came amongst us. Also different and special about Christmas Day was the good humour shown by the girls throughout the day. Once, when the toys were being distributed, there was a rush of boys up to the cabinet, which took me by surprise. I was last to be served, by which time all that remained was a balloon. Imagine my surprise when later I was

47

summoned to the Reverend Mother, who handed me a mouth organ. 'That's for being the only boy in the school to show some manners,' she said.

A visit from Santa Claus I knew to be something that happened only to outsiders, or 'rich' children. They were rich because they had parents and a home of their own. I reasoned that Santa, being a saint (St Nicholas), had no difficulty distinguishing between outsiders and children like us. Somehow, being orphans, we were unclean, inferior, and therefore undeserving of a visit. How madly I longed, how fervently I yearned for Santa Claus to come, just this once, but he didn't, which gives the lie to the old adage 'what you've never had you'll never miss'. Year after year we heard the same rumour, born of intense yearning, that this Christmas was different, Santa was definitely coming. And I believed it with all my heart. But Christmas morning yet again saw me crying tears of bitter disappointment – under the bedclothes, for fear of being seen and scoffed at by my playmates. Yet I admired their calm acceptance, and wished I could be more like them. They were advanced, more mature; I was still only in the process of learning that if you wished to avoid disappointments, you must have no expectations.

I thought of the 'rich' children who were visited by Santa Claus, and I envied them the other things they had too, and probably took for granted, things that would have meant so much to me – a home of my own, shared with my family, and all that that conjured up. Love headed the list, then a touch of fondness; protection and security from fear; an occasional hug and personal contact; a lap to sit on; a soft voice; a kind word; a sympathetic ear; a tuck-in at bedtime; a goodnight kiss. Not to have any of those as a little boy and to yearn for them as I did, constantly, was to know real heartache and rejection.

Ironically, we were learning in the school primer about young Peter's daily routine, blessedly so different from ours: how he came down each morning to breakfast prepared by his mother, then off with him to school on his own bicycle, but not without a goodbye kiss. An illustration showed his mother at the door welcoming Peter home in the evening, and Toby his little dog was there too, bouncing joyfully up to the garden gate to greet him. I envied Peter with all my heart.

6

FIRST HOLY COMMUNION AND
THE EUCHARISTIC CONGRESS

The happiest day of my five and a half years in the care of the
Sisters of Charity, apart from the day I left, was my First Holy
Communion Day, or to be precise the morning of that day, for
the day returned to normal after breakfast. Nuns being nuns, it
may be taken as read that they put the special class through a
great deal of arduous, meticulous preparation for our 'big day':
painstaking rehearsals, new prayers to learn, hymns to practise.
It also goes without saying that every care was taken by the
nuns to see that we were provided with new clothes, and splendid we all looked too, I'm sure. Alas, we must take all that for
granted, because those aspects of the big occasion have faded
from my memory forever, and I am truly sorry not to be able to
recount their detail now.

What I will never forget, however, and what eclipsed all
else about that day, was the special breakfast served to us First
Communicants at the top end of the refectory, separate from
the rest of the boys. Being thus set apart from the others was
very important in our eyes, for that is what gave us special
status for the day. The joyful anticipation began weeks before,
during which time popularity among our friends mounted apace
with their hopes that we'd give them a share of our Communion breakfast. That breakfast was the happiest experience of
my life until then, for instead of the usual bread and margarine,
we had fried bread. We knew of our breakfast menu in advance. It was the first year for it; all previous classes of First
Communicants had had a boiled egg!

I can still recall the sheer ecstasy of tasting the delicious
new flavours that surged from those juicy slices into my mouth
for the first time. Dish after dish of the succulent food was actu-

ally served to our table by two nuns in person, which added importance to the occasion. The rest of the refectory strained their necks to see the sight. Eagerly we reached out greasy, well-licked fingers for more, while the nuns asked in amazement where in the world we were putting it, but we were slyly sharing it with our friends, as promised. This was our special, long-awaited moment and we revelled in it, sustaining it as long as possible, until the nuns tired of the work. Such was the significance of my First Communion breakfast, such were the heights to which my joy and pleasure soared during the hour or so it lasted, that I can remember it vividly after seventy years, and yet (I am ashamed to confess) I have no recollection whatever of tasting the Blessed Sacrament for the first time.

Another memorable event was the International Eucharistic Congress, which took place in Dublin in June 1932. All the boys assembled in a large common room to listen to the wireless, purchased specially for the occasion. This was our introduction to the wireless, and when Sister Germaine explained just what the machine could do, we gazed in awe at the wonders of it. Hardly a day after that went by, however, without a breakdown, and an urgent summons to Mr Behan, to whom we appealed to get it going again. He would return as if about to burst a blood vessel, puffing and panting, staggering under the weight of a heavy battery almost as big as the wireless itself.

The Congress made a tremendous impact on the whole country, and photographs taken at the time, which I first saw decades later, were in many cases remarkably close to the mental pictures I drew from the wireless commentator's description of the vast crowds, the Papal Legate, Cardinal Lorenzo Laurie, the thousands of priests, bishops and nuns from all over the world, the colourful flags and bunting decorating every house in the city, and the seemingly endless processions of praying and hymn-singing people. The nuns and staff crowded the common room too, and they took a liking for one of the hymns we were hearing for the first time over the wireless. No one was surprised when 'Soul of My Saviour' was included in the chapel repertoire.

We were all affected by the solemn sanctity of the great event, carried away by religious fervour – and this from listening to it, seventy-five miles from the scene. What it must have been like to be there, I couldn't imagine. Countless decades of the rosary were recited by the vast crowds, and we, sitting cross-legged on the floor (the chairs were for nuns and the girls), could only stare in wonder at the modem miracle of the wireless, bringing responses to us from the throats of over a million people so far removed from us.

For all of us the climax to this most thrilling, uplifting experience was the personal address to the Irish nation broadcast direct from Vatican Radio by Pope Pius XI on the closing day. Nor was our amazement marred by the fact that we could hardly make out what he was saying, what with his strong Italian accent, and the heavy, crackling static and atmospheric interference. The mere fact of his speaking directly to us was enough to hold us spellbound.

My period in Miss O'Reilly's class stands out as probably the worst year I spent in Kilkenny. At a guess, Miss O'Reilly was in her late forties then. Sharp-featured and crabby, irascible and frightening, her facial expression suggested that she was constantly bringing up bile or suffering from heartburn. Whatever else she might be wearing, she never appeared without a multicoloured woollen hat clamped on the back of her head, which one boy aptly described as 'like a bumblebee's bum'. She taught all school subjects through terror, enforced by frequent smashes of the pointer on our hands.

She expected an instant response to a mental-arithmetic question, but in my case, fear of being wrong made me hesitate too long, from which she deduced (not always correctly) that I didn't know the answer. Thanks to her I developed a mental block for maths, which was to plague me for some years. I got many a severe beating, which left my fingers too sore to hold the pencil properly. This in turn caused me to be beaten again for having what she called 'sloppy writing'. I stormed heaven constantly, praying that the saints, my mother, my father – somebody, anybody at all – might shield me from her, but all my prayers fell on deaf ears. She terrified me. Years later I saw her double on the cinema screen, playing the part of Madame Defarge in *A Tale of Two Cities*, which didn't surprise me.

Once Miss O'Reilly deputised for Mr Behan in supervising our play period. The weather being bad that day, we stayed indoors. She got us to sit on the floor of the recreation hall as she walked among us reading stories about Little Red Riding Hood, Snow White and Hansel and Gretel. She probably meant well, but her own cross appearance and fearsome reputation added such realism that we became terrified, to such an extent that the danger from the wolf or witch or wicked queen which threatened the children in the stories became an equal threat to her listeners. Before long, many were trembling, in tears. When I remember how the stories scared the daylights out of me and my companions, I am amazed at how they came to be written at all, and why even today, in what is regarded as a more caring age, adults continue to regard as suitable for children these same tales, in which witches stuff little children into ovens, and wolves gobble up grandmothers.

In my final year I had to say goodbye to many of my chums; as it transpired, it was goodbye forever in most cases. They were scattered around the country, to Letterfrack in County Galway, Clonmel in County Tipperary, Upton in County Cork, and Carriglea and Artane in County Dublin, to name only some of the institutions. They were described variously as industrial schools, approved schools, or reformatories, and were managed by religious orders. While a boy had some claim to a school where his older brother was, and this was generally met, anyone else could find himself packed off to wherever there happened to be a vacancy, regardless of whether he might have a widowed mother or father anxious to visit him.

As my time to leave drew near, I was taken to be vaccinated. I spent ten horrible days in the infirmary, cocooned in bed, suffering the stench of my scabs and those of my companions, with, of course, the other features of the infirmary: thirst and intense heat. After our recovery, the others left, Joe Blackburn for Letterfrack and Trevor Mortimer for Artane, but I was detained.

Mother Otteran, the Reverend Mother, had a brother who was in the Dominican Order and who visited her at Easter. I was impressed by his white habit, and must have let my interest show somehow, for it was decided that I should be transferred to an orphanage run by that order. In a few days I was dressed in new clothes and taken to Dublin by Sister Ursula. I wasn't leaving quite yet, she said; I was going to be 'seen' by Father Dowling, the Superior of St Saviour's Orphanage, Dominick Street, Dublin. 'You'll be asked a lot of questions, I'm sure,' she said, 'but don't be afraid, and remember to speak up nice and loud, won't you? And for heaven's sake, smile,' she added with emphasis. 'Why must you go about like a sorrowful mother?' Placing me in the care of the Dominican Order was to be, I imagine, the first step in achieving her priestly ambition for me.

Sister Ursula was very nice and informal for a time on the train, and I remember thinking that she wasn't like a nun any more, but more like an ordinary person. She was unusually friendly and gave me fruit, some of which – plums, for instance – I had never tasted before. Nuns, it seemed, had to keep up an austere and haughty manner before the public. It was what people expected. Anything else would not be in keeping with their holy state. In the school we saw many signs of their human, friendly character, and this is what I now saw in Sister Ursula – while we were alone in the carriage. It was short-lived, however, and vanished when we were joined by other passengers.

At St Saviour's we were shown into the parlour while someone went to fetch Father Dowling. I took an instant dislike to the place. It was the aroma – the furniture-polish smell – that sent out the first warning and stoked up the embers of the memory of my traumatic arrival in Kilkenny. I felt the fear and apprehension that I had known before. And there were the visual signals too: the shiny mahogany furniture, the highly polished floor, the gloomy 'holy pictures' whose presence was felt more than seen in the half-light, because the only window in the room was heavily draped. Add a palpable silence, as the nun and I waited, and you will perhaps understand with what alacrity I reached the conclusion that this was no place for me.

Years later I would find this combination of sight and smell typical of the residential part of religious houses I chanced to visit in the course of business, and I would experience flashbacks of the same unease, discomfort and nervousness – echoes of a bygone fear. Presently I had a wonderful surprise as my mother came in, but since she was closely followed by Father Dowling, we had no time to embrace or talk to each other. As though deliberately to forestall that, the priest got down to business right away.

There was a lot of talk, and I looked from one face to another, not understanding what was being said. There was lengthy discussion about a fee of twelve pounds which, my mother firmly said, was 'out of the question'. Then Father Dowling said something to which my mother replied emphatically: 'That's different entirely. I couldn't afford to pay that amount, or indeed any fee at all, so there's nothing more to be said really.' As she reached for her handbag and gloves, she added, 'We're sorry to have wasted your time, I'm sure,' and my spirits rose.

The priest wasn't finished, and placed a hand on her arm to restrain her, before switching his attentions to me, enquiring about my health record. How often had I been ill in the infirmary? When I told him 'lots of times', he wanted to know what had been wrong with me. I answered as well as I could, with some help from Sister Ursula.

Then to her he said, 'His eyes are rather swollen . . . just here, underneath . . . don't you think?'

'No, I wouldn't say that at all – not really, they've always been like that.'

'Step over to the window and let me have a better look, boy,' said the priest, wishing, I'm sure, to prove his point. 'Chin up, there's a good lad . . . hmmm . . . ' Then, dropping his voice, he went on, 'This puffiness under the eyes – could be a sign of kidney trouble, if you ask me.' Out loud, he asked, 'Any problem with his kidneys, Sister?'

'Well, yes, now that you mention it, he did have a kidney infection once, but – '

'There, what did I tell you?' he said triumphantly.

'But it was only a minor one,' protested the nun. 'It soon cleared up. Besides, Father, it was over two years ago.'

'Mmm, well just the same ... I'm afraid that settles it, Sister. I'm sorry, but we couldn't accept the boy in the circumstances.'

And that was that. The finality in his tone left no room for pleadings, either from the nun or from my mother. To my great relief, Father Dowling rose and made for the door. We were dismissed. No cup of tea, not even for the nun in consideration of her long train journey. Hands were shaken, I was given an apple from a fruit bowl in the centre of the table, a pat on the head, and we were out the door within half a minute of the priest's decision.

Outside, my mother and Sister Ursula began talking quietly together. I heard the nun's opening remark, 'Sorry it didn't work out as I'd hoped, but that man ... ' and she allowed her voice to trail off on catching my eye. Later I managed to pick up a phrase – 'Carriglea School, it's the best of them' – which apparently pleased my mother very much. As she embraced me she said, 'You'll be going to Carriglea – you'll love it there, it's a great place. So much nearer, too, and I can see you oftener.' Then, placing her lips up close to my ear, she whispered, 'You'll be happier there, Joe, I promise.' How right she was.

The three of us set off by tram to Kingsbridge railway station, where I was put on a train to make the return journey on my own, the nun having arranged to stay at a city convent. The railway guard was instructed firmly to be sure and see that I got off at Kilkenny, and the order was issued with that air of authority which nuns could bring to bear so expertly on any situation, and which guaranteed compliance. For me, what would otherwise have been a tearful occasion – that of parting again from my mother – was in fact a happy one, because I knew I would soon be leaving Kilkenny for good.

7

GOODBYE KILKENNY

It was September 1933, and the day of my departure. At last! How often had I dreamt of this day, how many boys before me had I envied their last day! Now it was my turn.

I was ordered to have a bath and put on the clothes laid out for me in the washroom. I had a healthy boy's dislike for soap and water, and was on the point of saying, 'But I washed meself this morning, Sister', but thought better of it, knowing that it wouldn't have made any difference. 'And be quick about it, like a good boy,' the nun said, 'the taxi will be here in a few minutes.' Thank you, God. Thank you. I'm 'going away' (as it was known). Going away! I was flushed, trembling with happiness.

The washroom was empty of boys. Never before had I seen it like that. It was vast and hollow-sounding. Every movement of mine made a louder noise than usual, and echoed spookily round the walls. I felt a sort of fear. For the first time ever, I was going to have a bath on my own, without the screening companionship of the other boys, and I was afraid. Moreover, for the first time I was aware of my nakedness and strangely uneasy about it – shy, apprehensive and guilty. Being naked and alone in this expansive room was like being out in the open air with no clothes on, and it was this, I suppose, that brought feelings of guilt. Never when standing naked in the bath with other boys had I known such feelings, for we provided cover for each other. Now, on my own, I was shamefully exposed, ill at ease, and guilty – of what, I didn't know. Quickly scrambling into the bath lest the nun should come in and see me in this state, I sat well down in the water to hide my body, then began washing nervously, hurriedly, so as to get it over and done with as quickly as possible.

Deprived of our individuality by strict discipline and regimentation, and bonded by common hardship and privation, we had absolutely no inhibitions in anything we did. And we did everything together in response to the whistle or the bark of an order. Everything. We got up in the morning together, prayed, played, dined, went to classes, fell in, fell out and marched here, there and everywhere in double file. Heedless of considerations of modesty, we openly undressed for bed and bath. We defecated in toilets which had no cubicles or curtains to give even a modicum of privacy. We knew nothing about modesty, and even the girls in charge had scant regard for it, as when, for instance, they stripped down the bedclothes and raised a boy's shirt to cane his nakedness for talking in the dormitory, or for being awake. Modesty was a virtue we knew nothing about, but that ignorance would be remedied in my next school. There it would be a different story entirely – almost an obsession.

I dressed in the clothes I had worn to St Saviour's: a white short-sleeved shirt, grey short trousers, grey knee-length stockings with fold-down multicoloured tops, brown sandals with white 'soapy' soles and a dark-grey sleeveless jumper. I was ready to go. With a sudden crash the door burst open and in came Mr Behan, furious at seeing me already bathed and dressed. Roughly taking the collar of my shirt and folding it outside my pullover, he snarled, 'Will you take a look at the cut of you! I've seen tidier scarecrows. Is this the best you can do? Couldn't wait for me, could you? Eh? Eh?'

The dreaded repetition meant he expected an answer, and I had better offer one. Cringing, expecting a wallop, I bleated, 'If you please sir, the nun said I was to bath and change quick, and not keep the taxi man waitin'. I didn't know you were comin' . . . '

'And how do you think you're getting to Dublin, may I ask – on your own? For two pins I'd make you start all over again. Let me have a look at you then . . . Straighten those socks, for heaven's sake. Hmmm, I suppose you'll have to do. Have you gone to the yard?'

'No sir, I don't want – '

'Off with you at once; I know you only too well.' He raised his voice after me. 'And don't take all day!'

In the gravelled forecourt I stood waiting for the taxi that would take me to the station. I had no luggage; my sole possession, my prayer book, was in my pocket. I was over-flowing with joy. Never had I known such happiness. 'I'm leaving, I'm leaving,' I kept saying to myself. I wanted to shout it out. To sing. Something told me I'd be describing this moment in years to come, and I looked long and hard about me so that the scene would stay fresh in my mind.

Of the trees that skirted the forecourt and the chapel, I knew every branch and twig, it seemed. An affinity had grown between us during my daily task of sweeping the garden paths nearby – the same with the birds that I fed every day. Robins and wagtails I could identify, but there were others – wrens, thrushes and finches, I suppose. I loved them all. They were my companions of the garden, my secret friends in a happy oasis who gave me many a laugh, strutting brazenly to within a yard or two of me, showing off their bravery – but always flying away when I tried to lure them closer.

Just now I was too far away to see them, and I was disappointed. 'I'll miss them,' I thought to myself. 'But nobody else. Especially now that Joe White and other close chums have gone before me.' By rights I should have left in March, when I was ten, but I suppose efforts to place me in St Saviour's had delayed my going. 'Well, no matter, I'm leaving at last, and I don't care,' I thought. I was facing a new adventure – that's the feeling exactly, complete with doubts, fear and uncertainty about the future.

Presently Sister Ursula came to say goodbye. She was formal again, and severe. 'Maybe she's sorry I'm leavin' – or did I let her down by not gettin' into St Saviour's?' I wondered.

The arrival of Sister Victor interrupted me. 'Thank goodness you're still here, Joe,' she said. 'I was afraid I had missed you.' She didn't usually fuss, and now she was out of breath. I never saw her like this. She squeezed my shoulders and patted me on the head, and for a moment I thought she was going to kiss me. She pressed a small picture of Our Lady into my hand. 'For your prayer book,' she said, a suggestion of tears in her voice. 'Whenever you look at it, say a little prayer for me. I won't forget you, Joe, and don't you ever forget me, do you hear?' she said, with a brave attempt at a smile, for she was indeed on the verge of tears. I warmed to her at that moment as never before. She was easily the best, I thought. Unfortunately, I was never to see her again, or indeed any of the nuns I had known there.

Many years later I drove up the avenue, the tall trees flanking it now badly thinned by Dutch elm disease, and over I went to the side of the chapel to survey my flower garden. But it was no more. In its place was a small enclosure containing the graves of some of the nuns I had known – Mother Otteran, Sister Bertha, Sister Bega and poor blind Sister Coman. I entered and stood near them, and did not feel I was intruding. 'Of course not,' I thought. 'I'm among friends here.' I waited a while at each grave, my mind returning to some little incident linking us. I didn't call at the convent. Nobody would know or remember me after forty years.

The taxi arrived, and Sister Perpetua came rushing over, out of breath, her feet noisily crunching the gravel. Thrusting a brown paper parcel upon me, she said, 'There's lots of lovely things here for you to eat on the train. I made them up as a special treat. It's my own surprise for you. Think of me when you're enjoying them. Goodbye Joe, and please don't forget to pray for us all.' Sister Perpetua had been less than a year at St Patrick's when she overheard me referring to her as 'the new nun with the beautiful baby face', and I had become her special friend thereafter.

Two or three other nuns came at the last minute, and the group all began to talk at the same time, shaking hands with me, saying what a great boy I was, and how well I looked 'all dressed up'. I was fussed over and praised. This was so unreal and so out of character, nuns showering me with kindness, their haughtiness put aside. How should I react? Such a bonanza of good wishes, smiles and pats on the head confused me, so that I sought sanctuary in the taxi as speedily as I could. Up with me onto its running-board, then an awkward scramble and an ungainly sprawl across the leather upholstery. As I looked out upon the smiling nuns jostling for position, I thought, 'Why weren't ye this nice to me before? Why did ye leave it so long?'

Sister Vianny from the infirmary was the biggest surprise of all – my precious marble still in her pocket, I was sure.

My memory of St Patrick's as an emotionally harsh place has not dimmed in all the years since I left it, although to be fair I have to say that my long-term misery was attributable more to my homesickness and craving for love and kindness than to the occasional physical punishments I received, severe though they were. To be sure, it was not the nuns who inflicted the sometimes brutal punishments on their defenceless charges – that is to say, theirs was not the hand that wielded the rod. But we believed that the nuns had overall charge of the institution, and therefore approved of the regime. All the boys must have believed that, which would explain why no one complained about the behaviour of Mr Behan and some of the girls. The possibility of the nuns' being unaware of the behaviour of those they placed in charge didn't occur to us, and yet this was the case, as I was to learn later.

From the vantage point of old age, I can see how nuns in those far-off days came to be excessively zealous in devoting their lives to God, swathing themselves in black sanctity, secluded in their convent, in a world of their own. I now believe there was a lot of snobbish nonsense about the taking of the veil in the old days, which the laity helped to keep in place by showing excessive deference to the nuns, elevating them to a position just below the angels, or treating them like demigods. And the nuns thrived on the special status accorded to them.

Their general behaviour and their relations with everyone were characterised by an austere detachment which severely restricted communication with those to whom they had delegated responsibility, and formed a barrier between them and the children placed in their care. Someone in authority in the Church or state should have realised that such exclusivity was incompatible with the running of a home for children – as incompatible as oil and water.

Thankfully, Vatican II cleared that away. It brought nuns closer to lay people, encouraging them to work hand in hand with the laity, and on level terms. It humanised them, one could say. Also, I think abolishing the nuns' centuries-old garb contributed in no small way to bringing about the transformation we see today. To small children especially, the nun's habit was an ominous sign of her power and authority, and that of the Church she represented.

The state was more culpable, firstly for its policy of committing orphans of the poor so cruelly to institutions (with or without a surviving parent's consent), as though the object were to cleanse society of them; and secondly, for not having in place a follow-up mechanism whereby the welfare and treatment of the children was monitored. As it was, these institutions or homes were in the hands of religious orders exclusively, and in the climate of the time the state would not wish to be seen to question the orders' competence to manage them. Apart from committing the children, there was very little state involvement other than making a per capita payment to the school. What passed for monitoring was a visit by a schools inspector to examine the children's educational standards. He was a teacher with no qualifications in child welfare, paediatrics or medicine, and was therefore the wrong man for the job.

Undoubtedly through charitable motives, and for economic reasons also, the nuns employed poor, homeless, inexperienced girls to look after the children, in return for bed and board and probably little else. That these girls were unqualified, as well as intellectually and temperamentally unsuitable, was patently seen as of little consequence. Had there been occasional spot checks of the institutions by a competent official, the utter inappropriateness of the staff would have come to light, and the children would have been spared much misery. To my certain knowledge, no inspection was carried out during my five and a half years in St Patrick's Boys' Industrial School. In my second institution there was one inspection, but that was by an education inspector who was solely concerned with our education – or, to be precise, with one aspect of it, namely our knowledge of the Irish language!

The nuns' self-imposed remoteness from ordinary life in the school insulated them from its day-to-day routines; this explains how they knew nothing of the excessively harsh treatment meted out to their charges by Mr Behan and a few others. This complete unawareness may be hard for people nowadays to accept as plausible, not having seen how detached nuns could be from ordinary mortals in those far-off years before the Second Vatican Council. Even when travelling outside their convent, nuns were seen in pairs, their minds obviously on a higher plane, each softly muttering responses to her companion's prayers, and apparently oblivious to their surroundings.

A year after I left St Patrick's I learned from a boy newly transferred to Carriglea that Mr Behan had been sacked following an inquiry into his conduct set up by the Reverend Mother. Some boy had complained to her after all, and the ensuing questioning of all the boys exposed the cruelties that had been going on for years.

My attitude towards the nuns changed when I heard about Mr Behan's dismissal, for then I realised how wrong I was in assuming that they were aware of his behaviour and that they condoned it. It is part of my religious upbringing that without 'full consent and perfect knowledge' there is no fault. So I hold the nuns blameless.

It might be supposed that our harsh and cruel treatment in an institution run by a religious order would inevitably have laid within me the foundations of a deep, lasting hatred of religion, but strange to say, that is not so. In fact, it made me very pious. In abject misery and deep despair, I sought consolation in daily prayer. Inwardly, and without anyone being aware of it, I prayed to Christ and His mother. Who else was there to turn to? My only friends were among the other boys, and they were as impotent as I (although I doubt they were as miserable).

I prayed fervently – not only during formal prayer times, but informally in the ordinary course of the day. In the classroom between lessons I prayed with all my might that I would avoid Miss O'Reilly's painful attentions; elsewhere I prayed that I wouldn't fall foul of Mr Behan, or Kathleen, or Mary Jo. And praying did help. As I sometimes lay in bed trying to stifle my sobs, afraid of a jeering from the other boys, or a thrashing from the girl in charge if I was heard, I turned to prayer. Before long, and with a sense of immense relief, I slipped languidly into sleep.

To this day I pray regularly for the nuns: Reverend Mother Otteran, Sisters Germaine, Bega, Bertha, Martha, Perpetua, Ursula, Victor, Coman, Vianny, Imelda, Agnes and Senan. In fact, I still remember them with sincere affection. There were nuns whose names I have forgotten, and others whose names I never knew, but I remember their faces and pray for them all. What a pity they didn't involve themselves more with the boys – it would have made a world of difference to me.

8

JOURNEY TO DUBLIN

In the taxi on my way to the train station, a new school and a new life, my exhilaration and excitement grew apace with the distance from the convent. Swaying from side to side in the luxury of the car's upholstery, I thrilled to the feeling of speed, weaving in and out of Kilkenny's mainly horse-drawn traffic, effortlessly leaving it behind.

What little other motorised traffic there was consisted chiefly of large, square, cumbersome vans and lorries. Horses, yoked to their carts, stood patiently outside the shops, munching oats in nosebags, awaiting their owners' return. Nearly every shop had a canvas awning that sloped over the footpath to shade windows from the sun. Hundreds of people crowded the footpaths, some randomly crossing the streets – pedestrian crossings and traffic lights were not even dreams of the future in those far-off days. 'It's just like Dublin,' I thought, and I meant it as a compliment. Unfortunately, this, my second or third car ride ever, came to an end all too soon and we came to the station.

With a firm grip on my parcel, I walked beside Mr Behan up the slope to the railway station and ticket office. 'We're in plenty of time,' he told me as he ordered me to sit on a wooden bench parallel to the tracks. 'Don't stir from there till I get back; I'm only going to the bookstall. And don't dare open that parcel until we're on the train.'

Sitting on my own, I became greatly interested in everything around me, marvelling wide-eyed at the general activity, the hustle and bustle increasing by the minute. The supremacy of the train in the world of transport had not yet been seriously challenged by the motor car in the Ireland of 1933, so the railway station of a large town was a bustling place indeed. It soon filled up with earnest people rushing about in search of something or somebody. Others, standing expectantly in little groups, unconcernedly blocked the way – men with waxed moustaches, their topcoats folded across their arm, women in long loose coats with fur collars or stoles. Hats seemed compulsory wear for grown-ups then; bowlers were favoured by most of the men. A pile of luggage – metal chests, mostly – grew larger by the minute as shirt-sleeved porters stacked more of them on the platform.

On the far side, a carriage-less engine persisted in attracting my attention, shunting importantly back and forth like a steamroller, chuffing and puffing and belching out steam. 'Over here, over here,' it seemed to say, undecided whether to go or stay. It might have been staging a show for me; no one else paid the slightest attention. I'd have gladly sat there all day long, drinking in the sights and sounds, but all too soon, with a farewell flourish on its whistle, it made its exit off the stage.

With the first faint sound of an approaching train way off from the side came a general movement of people towards the edge of the platform. My excitement peaked a moment later when, with an earth-shaking din, the train for Dublin snorted in.

Soon everyone seemed to be boarding – everyone but me. I stood on the bench to try to find Mr Behan, but among the sea of bobbing faces his was not to be seen. It was hard to see clearly with so many people scurrying this way and that. There was such an air of panic, I became infected with it.

'If he doesn't hurry, I'll be left behind,' I thought. 'Then what will I do?' In no time at all, as if by magic, the crowd thinned out, then vanished entirely, vacuumed into the train. Yet there was still no sign of Mr Behan. I was in a real panic now. Jumping down from the bench, I scampered across to the nearest carriage, deciding to wait no longer. I would not be left behind. Yet I stopped short of actually boarding, for I wasn't used to doing anything without permission. The railway guard, walking pompously by, paused in his job of banging the doors shut to ask in a gruff voice what was I hanging about for, and did I want to go or didn't I? This brought me to the verge of tears.

At last Mr Behan, panting hard, rushed up, coming from nowhere, it seemed. He bundled me up on board ahead of him, and both of us flopped onto the nearest seat, just in time. Doors slammed, someone shouted, a whistle blew, but that wasn't the end of the commotion. The train lurched away with tremendous belches of black, soot-laden smoke and a frightening roar far worse than before. Thrown fully back in my seat, my legs in the air as we gathered speed, I was thrilled and immensely relieved.

But my relief was short-lived. Not until we were under way, when it was too late, did I discover that I had left Sister Perpetua's parcel on the bench behind me in the station. I couldn't keep the tears from welling into my eyes, nor control their flow. I was shattered. This was the very moment that I was to open my parcel and feast on its delights. The eager anticipation I had barely managed to control until now evaporated with amazing speed. In its place was a gloomy sense of loss. I settled down to brood on my misfortune, imagination running unbridled as to the mouth-watering contents of the lost parcel, and I seemed to revel in self-torture. For one accustomed for years to a daily dinner of stew, and for breakfast and supper a never-varying diet of bread and margarine, to have a veritable feast snatched from his lips was almost impossible to bear. Indulging my child's imagination to the full, the parcel's contents increased in quantity and lusciousness by the minute. It contained everything delicious one could possibly imagine, and in huge amounts too, but it never occurred to me to wonder how I could have managed to carry it from the taxi if that were really true.

I was talking about it months afterwards to my new friends. 'There was bags of sangwidges,' I told them, 'ham an' beef an' all, an' curran'y cake, an' buns, an' jam tarts, an' d'yez know that yellow cake that has no currants or nothin' in it?'

'Madeira?'

'Yeah, that. An' as for fruit – oh, loads of apples, oranges, pears an' grapes, bananas, an' even plums. Did any of youse ever taste plums before?'

'Millions o' times.'

'So did I. Smashin', aren't they?'

'Any sweets?' asked one, eyes widening by the minute.

'Sweets? Will yeh hold yer patience, sure amn't I comin' to them. Choc'lates, an' jellies, an' car'mels too, an' fizz bags, an' bull's-eyes an' all. Not forgettin' lemonade an' Vimto as well – six huge bottles, doncha know. D'yez know what I'm goin' to tell yez? It woulda taken me weeks to eat it, even givin' half of it to youse.'

'Fancy forgettin' a parcel the like o' that, the dirty-lookin' eejit!' came a voice laden with disappointment. 'Yeah! How could ye forget it?' came another. I didn't answer. That was my problem now – I couldn't forget it.

Apart from the ticking-off he gave me for 'stupidly forgetting "our" parcel,' and 'could I not be trusted on my own for one minute?' Mr Behan didn't speak for the rest of the journey. A lady opposite, assuming that I was unaccompanied, offered me some plums after a while. She asked if I was going on my holidays, and not understanding the term, I didn't know how to reply. Then remembering how, years before, when travelling to St Patrick's, my mother had told me that I was going on my holidays, I answered, 'Yes ma'am, I'm going to a new school.' The lady laughed heartily.

To a ten-year-old boy with his nose flattened against the window of a speeding train, the countryside is fascinating. And when it happens to be only the third or fourth train-ride of his whole life, there are no bounds to his exultation. So many things to see at once, and quickly too, or else they'll disappear from view: stacks of hay, ricks of wheat or corn, fields of green, brown and saffron – a huge patchwork bedspread, bramble-stitched, stretching for miles and miles to the vague hills in the distance; all this and more, seen through the railings of flying telegraph poles, their mesh of wires aloft, sagging and rising, sagging and rising, with an almost hypnotic effect. The only signs of life were

69

a few horses or cattle and some crows. 'No people; they won't appear until the next station. The rest of the passengers have fallen asleep. I'm alone,' I thought.

No train journey since has been as exciting as that one. I often wondered what thrilled me so much on that particular day. It could hardly have been the fleeing landscape alone. Perhaps it was a mixture of that and the excitement of speed, coloured by high expectations of what lay ahead for me, although admittedly some twinges of foreboding were present, even though my new school had a good reputation among the boys. In contrast to that journey, I find now that there's nothing like a monotonous landscape, and the accompanying clackety-clack of a train, to lull one into a sound sleep.

We stopped at some small stations to pick up a passenger or two. The routine, I noticed, was always the same: the guard strolled the length of the train, calling out the station's name, then ambled leisurely back to the rear, with all the time in the world to spare, slamming shut a door or two. We chuff-chuffed on our way again, with blasts of noise and smoke and grime, leaving behind a statuesque railway porter gazing abstractedly after us.

At long last, subtle changes intruded in the landscape: some houses, singly at first and then in terraces, backs to the railway line; then a spread of housetops and chimneys with a ribbon of road below, for we had been rising imperceptibly. The sound of the train was changing – it was fainter, less enclosed, less muffled than before, as the permanent way broadened out in a wide expanse of multiple track. From these signs I guessed we were near Dublin.

By some instinct the grown-ups sensed it too, coming to life together and reaching overhead for coats and hand luggage. The train slowed and chuff-chuffed into Kingsbridge station, bent on making as big a commotion as possible. In an undertone, with a veiled threat behind it, Mr Behan snapped at me to stick close to him and be sure I didn't get lost, adding that we still had a long way to go.

We went by electric tram from Kingsbridge along the course

of the Liffey, on which beer-barrelled barges put-put-putted along, intending to transfer their cargo of Guinness to a large ship berthed outside the Custom House. When it reached a bridge, each barge lowered its funnel on a hinge to allow it to pass under, amid clouds of black, sooty smoke that belched rudely upwards into curious faces peering from above.

We got off at O'Connell Bridge, which I recognised from memory, and near which, on Aston Quay, stood the terminus of red IOC buses which served the provincial towns. Crossing to the other side, over a mesh of tramlines set in cobblestones, we regained the Liffey wall, and further on came to the loopline and another railway station, smaller by far than the last. The view on the next train ride chiefly featured the sea and crowded beaches, for it was a warm, sunny day. In expecting another long journey, I was disappointed. It seemed that no sooner were we seated comfortably than we were at our destination, the coastal town of Kingstown, eight miles south of the capital, a town that I would know and love under its ancient name of Dún Laoghaire.

From here on we walked, and what a long walk it was to be. Soon I was near to tears from blistered heels inflicted by my new sandals. Round every bend, behind every corner, I expected my new school to come into view. Another ugly grey building, I supposed (I'd know it when I saw it, I was sure). But time and time again I was disappointed. 'This is unbelievable,' I thought. 'Fancy having to walk all this way.' Something prompted the idea that Mr Behan should have hired a taxi but had decided to walk instead and keep the fare for himself, and young as I was, I was quite annoyed. I was convinced that the nuns would not have expected us to walk all this way, particularly since they had ordered a taxi from the convent to Kilkenny station, which was but a fraction of this distance. The September day was oppressively warm now, and this didn't help one bit. And besides, we were lost. Several times a passer-by was asked for directions, and each time my hopes rallied on hearing the now familiar phrase, 'It's no distance at all from here, sure you can't miss it.'

Eventually we stood before a high double-gate, although there was no name to confirm it as our destination, nor any sight of a school building beyond. Up a long gravelled avenue we went. It was lined on each side by white railings, the slope becoming steeper. Halfway up, I heard a faint sound of children at play. I looked around eagerly, but couldn't locate its source. It appeared to come from every direction, and the further we walked, the louder and more diffuse it became. It was sweet music to my ears, and comforting, my nervousness allayed by its soothing sounds. No single voice dominated, nor were any words discernible in the chorus. The apprehensions, qualms and doubts that had gnawed at me on the train were magically dispelled; among such happy sounds there was no room for them. Enjoyment, high spirits, excitement, playful exuberance: all these commingled in full-throated harmony. I am haunted by the sound even now.

Today, seventy years on, when I'm out walking and I happen to be near a school during recess, I am ineluctably drawn towards the joyful sound of the children at play. In every respect it is the same sound that I heard in 1933. It is as though it never faded, never died, and from somewhere in the firmament it sends down echoes to remind me of my long-lost companions from that distant yesterday. I wrote this poem to express my love of the sound of children playing:

There is no sound to equal it Below,
Sweet music of the children as they play.
Oh may I hear it everywhere I go!

Surpassing every symphony I know,
'Twould even beat Beethoven's any day.
There is no sound to equal it Below.

Its chorus rings through Heaven to and fro,
(No pleasant sound is ever lost, they say).
Oh may I hear it everywhere I go!

Echoes still fond memories bestow,
Of playmates from a distant yesterday.
There is no sound to equal it Below.

Its absence, one of Hell's worst pains, and so
Is borne by tortured souls condemned to stay.
Oh may I hear it everywhere I go!

And when at last I reap what I did sow,
My prayer dear Lord is: 'After Judgment Day,
Since there's no sound to equal it Below,
Please, may I hear it everywhere I go?'

9

Carriglea School and The Brothers

A large mansion occupied the top of the avenue, a gravelled forecourt in front of it. Half a dozen wide steps led up to the main door, which was almost hidden beneath a portico supported by white pillars. This was Carriglea Park Industrial School, Dún Laoghaire. We didn't mount the steps; Mr Behan knew where to go. Hadn't he escorted many boys before – no doubt by taxi, or he'd have known the route from the station.

There would be no formal reception in the parlour, and I was glad. Instead, through a wicket gate we found ourselves in a large playground filled to capacity with laughing, running, playing boys. I was back with my own kind again. Children, children everywhere. They filled the lower yard where I was now, and a higher yard that lay up a flight of stone steps. In addition, beyond in the fields, a football match was in full swing. Never had I seen or heard the like. It was exhilarating.

We went over to the boys, Mr Behan and I, and they parted slightly to let us move through the crowd towards the Brother in charge, who at the same time advanced towards us until we met in a clearing the boys formed. 'Mr Behan, isn't it? We meet again,' the Brother said in that shy way he had with strangers which I would come to know so well later. They shook hands and moved away. A few boys drifted shyly towards me: the sheer numbers unnerved me and I timidly tried to keep my distance. One by one they made themselves known and reminded me who they were. They had come from Kilkenny too, they said, a year or two ahead of me. 'Don't you remember me?' 'And me?' asked another. 'There's loads of us here that you should know, there's him over there, and look at him, and remember so-and-so?'

The Price brothers came over and quickly put me at ease.

'This place is far better than Kilkenny. Wait till you see, you won't believe it. The Brother talking to Behan is Brother George. You'll like him. He's great.'

A senior boy was detailed to take Mr Behan to the kitchen for a cup of tea, and as I watched, I realised gratefully that I'd never see him again. Brother George took me aside. His black soutane, the broad sash around his waist and his black felt hat were off-putting, but his shy manner and soft, friendly voice reassured me.

'You're Joe Dunne, aren't you?'

'Yes Father,' I answered timidly, noticing his narrow clerical collar.

'You don't have to call me Father, I'm not a priest. I'm a Christian Brother. "Sir" will do fine.'

A few questions about my family background, and some spelling and arithmetic tests, told him all he wanted to know. 'Fine, very good,' he said. 'You're a grand lad. Don't be nervous. Come to me if you've any problem.'

Carriglea Park Industrial School
(Photo by Edward Dunne, courtesy of Dún Laoghaire
Institute of Art, Design and Technology)

All the boys were dressed in black, except for an Eton collar of white celluloid. Their trousers reached below the knee; in fact, I was to learn that it was an offence to wear them short. Knee-length stockings and hobnailed boots completed the sorry uniform. Older boys wore unsightly 'plus twos': trousers that buttoned below the knee and were overlapped by long stockings, so that no part of the leg was exposed.

I was put in the charge of a senior boy named John Keogh who would be my monitor. A monitor had charge of a 'division' comprising sixteen boys, and there were seventeen divisions. The monitor's function was mainly to oversee his table at mealtimes and to count heads at 'fall in'. 'Come to me when the whistle blows,' he said, 'I'm on me way to band practice now.' And off he went.

'Have I missed me dinner?' I called after him. He turned, and walking backwards from me, shouted, 'No. You'll hear the bugle call.'

'Bugle call?' I asked.

'I suppose you know we have a band here?' someone said.

'Yes, my mam – mother told me. I'd love to join.'

'You don't join, you get picked. Us three are training in it – Willie, Peter and me. They also teach you a trade – whichever one you want: tailoring, shoemaking or farming.'

I learned later that carpentry had formerly been taught by Brother Ephraim, who was now living in retirement in the school. I soon got to know Brother Ephraim. Occasionally he gathered a small group to show them how to sharpen and use carpenter's tools. The exercise was a one-off and lasted only a week or so. How to make tongue-and-groove was as far as it went. In short, a small skill came the way of a few boys who were in the right place at the right time.

At first he could remember my name only when I told him – and then he remembered it well, of course! He was friendly and easily accessible, with a stock of funny stories. Although he repeated them often, we laughed every time, not wishing to disappoint him. Yet our laughter was genuine – yes, and hearty

76

too, since we only had to look at his face, folded up into all its wrinkles like a concertina, hissing sounds coming from his almost closed lips accompanied by loads of bubbles, his shoulders heaving up and down. If that didn't make you laugh, nothing would. Sometimes we didn't get the gist of a story, but we guessed it was finished when we saw him laughing heartily, for he thoroughly enjoyed his own stories. Down the years I was repeatedly reminded of Brother Ephraim when I saw the jolly face of 'Mick McQuaid' on tins of pipe tobacco.

He wore tiny rimless glasses clipped to his nose, and seldom looked through them. At Sunday evening religious class he would suddenly stop to allow his gaze to follow a fly, its flight slowed by a piece of thread which some boy would have tied to its legs. In disbelief he would clean his spectacles in his handkerchief, pinch them back on his nose, and look over them again without comment.

Brother White ran the large farm with the help of a dozen boys, and together they made the school self-sufficient. The boys were strong country lads who had chosen farming as a career and would go to private farms when they left school. Brother White was of stocky build, as broad as he was long, and spoke with the strangest of accents. It was English definitely – some said from Devon or Cornwall, others, that he was a cockney. It was nearly impossible to understand what he said. A favourite prank played on a new boy was to get him to ask Brother White to read aloud his letter from home. The puzzled look on the little lad's face was a howl to see as he stood in front of the Brother, not understanding a word the man was saying. The pranksters of course were well behind the Brother, hugely enjoying the joke.

When I came to Carriglea, Brother Benignus was the Superior. His tall, erect bearing and stern, austere appearance didn't encourage familiarity, and since he had little contact with the boys, that suited us. Usually he seemed preoccupied by important matters, but when occasionally he relieved a Brother in class, he was quite friendly. We saw him at morning Mass and evening prayers and sometimes in between, when, with dignity and aristocratic mien, he walked across the playground to his office in the upper yard. The boys opened a path respectfully to let him through, unlike the other Brothers, who always had a small group of hangers-on around them. Cardinal Pacelli, who became Pope Pius XII a few years later, might have modelled himself on Brother Benignus. A year or so after I arrived in Carriglea, Brother Benignus left us on transfer; not long afterwards we heard that he had been killed when crossing the road near the new Foxrock church.

Brother George succeeded him as Superior, a job he took on in addition to his normal responsibilities. We had a healthy respect for Brother George. We saw a lot of him in the course of the day: he supervised our getting up in the morning, our ablutions, bed-making, prayers, meals, and most of our recreation times. He also had charge of the senior dormitory from eight o'clock till lights out at nine. He was soft-spoken, caring and shy, and yet, probably to uphold his authority, he maintained a stern outer appearance. Even so, he was well liked, although he was wise to every trick. Some said he had eyes at the back of his head; others, that he could be in two places at the same time. Nothing escaped his notice, and only a fool would try to outsmart him. To keep nearly three hundred boys under control needed a firm grip on the reins, so when discipline was called for he could be severe, though not excessively so. Like some of the other Brothers, he used a leather strap on the hands, only he had a knack of making us feel that he was more upset than we were. What was upsetting for me was falling from his grace and favour. He avoided corporal punishment whenever possible, in favour of a public scolding or 'telling off'. Sarcasm was his strong suit, and small wonder that we dreaded the 'telling off' more than the strap. To those around, it caused amusement, to the victim, embarrassment and shame.

Tommy Nolan, who later became an army sergeant, reminded me years afterwards of the time when he was the victim of this Brother's sarcasm. Tommy was ordered to empty out the pockets of his jacket and to describe his 'valuables' for all to hear. He produced 'a tennis ball with the fluff worn off, for playing handball with; a spinning top that cost me tuppence; a bundle of cigarette cards in an elastic band; bootlaces; a few marbles; a letter from me mother; a mouth organ; a box of boot polish; half a bottle of Lucknow Sauce; a few screws an' nails; a flash lamp that cost one an' three; an' five stones for playin' jack-stones with.'

'Is that the lot?' the Brother demanded. 'You wouldn't by chance have left something behind, like a stepladder for instance?' There was great laughter. That was the code we lived by. Any of us might be the next victim, so we gave as good as we got. The Brother continued, 'Do you know what you remind me of? A jackass coming home from the bog with his panniers stuffed with turf.' We all guffawed loudly at Tommy's expense, even though our pockets were equally crammed. This was because we kept our personal things in an attaché case under our bed but weren't allowed access to them by day. In the morning, therefore, we filled our pockets with whatever items might be needed for the day's play.

My first teacher was Brother Duncan, who was young, popular and easy to get on with. He didn't use the strap but had a deadly aim with the blackboard duster, which landed on your desk from straight overhead, showering you with a cloud of chalky powder. That, and the laughter of your classmates, brought you back from your daydreams. Thanks to this Brother, I now looked forward to school every day, and began to make progress for a change. Then a strange thing happened: he did not turn up for class one day, and the whispering began when Brother George took over instead. There were all kinds of rumours, the general one being that he had 'dropped dead that morning'. The true cause of his absence was stranger still. He had left, not only the school, but the Christian Brothers order as well. We were shocked.

He was replaced by Brother Comerford. From the same mould as Brother Duncan, this man was young, ginger-haired and bursting with enthusiasm. The Irish language and Irish history were his strong subjects, and soon became our favourites. He wrote a play in Irish, set in the Williamite period of history, and we staged it for the school. I played the role of a Frenchman, General Lauzun, but because I tried to say my lines with a French accent, I almost lost the role. Irish was sacred. He gave priority to the spoken language. Writing it would come soon enough, followed by the rules of grammar. 'That's how you acquired English,' he said. 'Before you heard about verbs, nouns and tenses, you spoke English reasonably well. You can learn Irish the same way.' And it worked. We became fluent speakers of Irish, and every boy in the class was awarded the silver *fáinne* by examiners from the city. The *fáinne* was a silver ring worn by speakers of Irish in their lapel to encourage the spread of the language. We never progressed to the gold one, however, because of what happened next. It appears that the Brother had not obtained Department of Education approval for his method. We had a visit from a schools inspector named Proinnsias Ó Súilleabháin who became furious at our lack of knowledge of Irish grammar. He frothed at the mouth and went berserk in the classroom. He took the Brother to task in front of us, and ordered him to concentrate on grammar in future. And he did. It killed our interest in the subject stone dead.

There was one thing I didn't like about Brother Comerford. When he had charge of us in the junior dormitory, he pretended to hear someone talking, and as a punishment ordered 'Lights out!' so that he was then free to play hurling in the field on fine summer evenings.

'Right, that's it,' he'd say, just as we had turned into bed. 'I warned ye there was to be dead silence, but as usual, there's a chatterbox somewhere.' No one would have spoken at all, but we knew better than to protest. Once we did so, only to hear: 'Very well, just for that there'll be no reading in bed tomorrow also.'

It was still broad daylight at eight o'clock in summer, so 'Lights out' was only a signal to put books away, lie down and go to sleep. The wireless extension from the senior dormitory was switched off too. To rub salt in the wound, from the field outside, the crack of the Brother's hurley against the sliotar could be heard clearly, and it tantalised us as we lay in bed.

Brother Arthur shared the job of monitoring us with Brother Comerford, each being in charge for a month at a time. In his fifties, Brother Arthur was the oldest in the school, apart from a few Brothers who were living in retirement there. With his steel-rimmed spectacles pushed up on top of his head, he ambled between the long rows of beds, reading to us some exciting adventure story for an hour. Such was the silent, rapt attention we gave his every word that his voice, which was not particularly strong, could be heard by every boy in the ninety-yard-long dormitory. Of the books he read for us, the most memorable for me were *Robinson Crusoe*, *Treasure Island* and *Eric, or Little By Little*. *Treasure Island* was the most popular. We lay on our backs, hands under our heads, enthralled by the story unfolding; we stared at the ceiling but saw well beyond it, and lived each adventurous moment. When the session was nearing its end, we'd be holding our breath – would the Brother once more turn back from the door, or turn the lights down and say, 'That's where we'll leave it; it's time now for sleep. Tomorrow's another day.'

The following day we'd be trying to guess what direction the story was going to take. 'Do you think the young fella – ye know, yer man, "Jim Hawkins" – will be discovered hidin' in the barrel?'

'Naw, no chance.'

'Don't be so sure. I think he'll be spotted by the parrot, who'll snitch to Long John Silver. Betcha what you like.'

'How much?'

'Hundred pounds.'

'Ye're on.'

10

DAILY ROUTINES

We were awakened at half past six every morning by Brother George walking up and down between the rows of beds ringing a handbell, and calling any boy he thought was not quick enough. We were expected to jump out of bed right away, without delaying even to stretch or scratch. The tardy ones were told to 'see me later'; persistent 'lazybones' were slapped. After a quick douse of cold water on our faces to freshen up – having had a thorough wash the night before, no more was necessary – the Brother blew his whistle. This was the signal to assemble in the lower playground, where each boy joined his division, whose monitor 'counted heads'. Then we double-filed into the chapel for seven o'clock Mass and Benediction, celebrated by our young chaplain, Father Sylvester Burke. The Mass was drawn out, probably to fit our daily schedule, so it was hard to keep praying for nearly a whole hour. The priest had little involvement with us, but being an altar boy I knew him better than most.

Daily Mass didn't draw us closer to God, as was intended, because of its length and also because we did not go of our own free will. There were two exceptions: Seán Quinn grew up to be a parish priest in Canada, and Patrick Donaldson joined a priestly order in Holland. The rest of us eagerly looked forward to Wednesday, when there was no Mass and we could enjoy an extra hour in bed.

After Mass it was back to the dormitories to remake our beds. Responding to the whistle at every stage, we stripped the beds and piled blankets and linen on the floor, then, taking each item in turn, we gave it a thorough shaking before spreading it on the bed again. The sash windows on both sides of the dormitory were open during this operation. We finally smoothed away any wrinkles from the bed's surface and stepped back to allow for a quick inspection.

On a rare occasion a boy wet his bed, and my heart went out to him in sympathy, because he had to run the gauntlet through the long rows of beds to the top of the dormitory with his bed linen, then back again with fresh replacements, all to the merciless jibes and jeers of the boys. Although I hadn't experienced it, I pitied the poor lads who did, and I had nightmares about it happening to me. In fact I saw it as the worst possible mishap. In my recurring dream I was dressed only in a short shirt, which, to make matters worse, kept flapping up behind me as I made my shameful journey through endless rows of jeering boys towards the linen cupboard, which kept moving further and further away.

Mealtimes were proclaimed by a bugle call from the band's solo cornet player, Charlie Wynne, who stood at various vantage points, such as the approaches to playing fields and farm. There were different bugle calls for each occasion, some just to announce the time.

For breakfast we had a mug of tea, poured from large metal containers by the 'kitchen wallopers', two or three boys who helped the adult male cook in the kitchen. Every group of four boys shared a loaf of bread and a dessert dish of melted dripping. You'd cut your quarter loaf into two-inch slices and gently lower each onto the dripping, barely deep enough to cover the surface. This was done under the close scrutiny of the boys with whom you shared the bowl. The monitor settled any arguments. On Fridays, instead of dripping, we had margarine, meat in any form being forbidden by the Church.

What we called 'lunch' was a short break at half past eleven. We assembled in the lower playground for a piece of dry bread two inches thick, distributed from large wicker baskets by a kitchen helper, with no tea, milk or even water to wash it down. We ate it where we stood, out in the open, even in winter. Brother Ephraim said this was our most beneficial meal, since the absence of something to drink obliged us to 'masticate the bread thoroughly'. The break was only long enough for its purpose; there was no playtime afterwards. For its bread supplies, the school divided its custom between three bakeries: Bolands' and Peter Kennedys' of Dublin, and Kennedys' of Cabinteely. The Cabinteely bread was disliked by some because of its sour taste, and preferred by others for the same reason. The school wanted to support the local firm, so the grumblers were ignored.

Dinner at three consisted of soup in a mug, four potatoes in their jackets, minced beef and cabbage. The potatoes were very moist and soapy, probably from having been steamed, but were no less palatable for that. The beef was cooked in huge copper cauldrons before being minced in a large electric mincer, a process which pressed away all the meat's juices, leaving behind dehydrated, hard pellets which were not easily swallowed. The cabbage was always green, leathery, poorly strained and, I may add, inedible. The soup was simply the water in which the meat had been boiled, with nothing added or taken out. I said we had a mug of soup; to be accurate, we were served with it. But since to drink it meant first having to consume half an inch of grease on its surface, it was always left untouched. Not even the ravenous appetites of healthy boys could rise to it – or to the cabbage. After dinner, these leftovers, with the potato skins and scraps, were wheeled down to the farm for the pigs. Even though the refectory was supervised by Brother George or the Master, no comment was passed about the rejection of soup and greens every day. However, we did have plenty of meat and potatoes to keep our healthy appetites at bay.

Sometimes, as a surprise and welcome treat, there was sausage meat instead of minced beef for dinner. Afterwards it was a great privilege for a chosen few to be allowed into the kitchen to chip off the dried sausage meat on the sides of the cauldrons. The Brother selected a different group of boys each time for this. Dinner on Friday had an element of uncertainty and sometimes of surprise because, in addition to the standard bread and margarine, there might be jam, or cheese, or maybe a dish of custard. As with the sausage meat, we would ask with up-

84

raised hands to be allowed to help ourselves to the scrapings of dried custard afterwards.

Supper was the same as breakfast, except for those who had money to supplement theirs with 'extras', having pre-arranged with someone to buy the extras in the village, or in Dún Laoghaire. I later had a role in the buying of extras, as I will relate presently. It was not uncommon for a boy to mix an Oxo cube into his tea, which was already sugared and milked, and into this liquid he would mash his bread. I tried this concoction myself, and it was good. I suppose the fact that it differed from what the others were having gave it added relish. In any case, a boy did not have much left for himself when he had given many others a taste. Sharing everything was a code of practice we grew up with from the beginning, and was done automatically. It was so much part of our lives that it's difficult to avoid repeating the fact throughout my narrative.

Lucknow Sauce was also a favourite teatime extra. We spread it on the bread and dripping, and while eating it we stared in fascination at the label on the bottle. This portrayed a turbaned Indian servant boy holding a tray or salver on which stood a bottle of Lucknow Sauce, whose label depicted an Indian boy holding a similar tray with a bottle of sauce, displaying an Indian boy whose tray . . . and so on into infinity. We tried to count the Indian boys as they diminished in size to a final speck, each of us arriving at a different total.

The money to procure these purchases was obtained from the boys' 'people' on Visiting Sunday. My mother could not afford to visit, but she wrote occasionally, enclosing six red penny postage stamps with their 'sword of light' motif, which Brother George cashed for me. I had by this time outgrown my obsessive longing for mother and home, and was thoroughly enjoying my stay with the Brothers, so I didn't envy the other boys their visits from relatives. The occasional letter quite satisfied me – with its sixpence worth of stamps inside, of course. I also earned a bit by selling sweets in the school shop at a commission of a few pence per box.

Before tea we filed into the chapel for evening prayers, which consisted of the rosary and litany, led by the Brother Superior. All the Brothers came as well. Surprisingly, although we had energy to burn in the playground, the moment we arrived in the chapel we were exhausted, aching to sit down. But we had to remain kneeling, endlessly. If we didn't become saints, it wasn't the Brothers' fault.

At a quarter to eight we repaired to the washroom, for every night we washed head, legs and feet in cold water at the wash-basins. The Brother quipped light-heartedly: 'Come on now, Joe, get into those ears and wash them' or 'Wash off that high-water mark from your neck, Tony, like a good lad' or 'The soap won't bite you, use plenty of it'. We were expected to maintain a good standard of personal cleanliness and a tidy appearance. Should a boy happen to be dirty or sloppily dressed he was called a 'muck ball' and ordered to report to his monitor, from whom he got a telling off, or a clip in the ear if no one was look-ing. A boy with a stocking round his ankle was said to have it 'at half-mast' and would be ordered to fix it right away. He'd be seen afterwards going around the playground, begging: 'E'er a bit o' twine or a spare shoelace?' so that he could tie it in place.

Each boy had his own toothbrush, the handle of which bore his name in Indian ink. (Every item of our clothes bore a label marked in the same way.) We didn't bother with toothpaste, and used the 'dirt shifter' soap we washed ourselves with, foul-tasting though it was. When night ablutions were finished, every boy collected an enamel chamber pot, or 'night vessel', which he placed under his bed. It was used when passing water only – otherwise, the toilets had to be visited. When using his night vessel, a boy had to kneel close to his bed with the vessel well underneath it, so as to preserve the maximum modesty. Even so, he had to wait until after lights-out in case, by a remote chance, any part of his lower torso might be visible.

We slept in the shirt we had worn during the day, and which was changed only on weekends. It reached to the knees, and opened with three buttons near the neck to allow your head through. While you dressed and undressed, you had to be very careful that your waist was fully covered; an accidental lapse got you a sharp slap and a warning. Singlets and underpants were unknown even in the coldest weeks of winter, when we could have done with them. Dormitories and classrooms were cold places indeed, their small turf fires producing nothing but smoke.

Obsession about modesty permeated all areas in the school, and even influenced the games we played. For instance, certain games, such as leapfrog and piggybacks, were banned entirely; they were considered immodest because a boy had to bend over when playing them. Again, strict silence had to be observed in the toilets and environs in case, no doubt, the surroundings might evoke immodest talk. Any offender in this regard got a severe slapping, however innocuous his breach of the rule might have been.

Modesty was paramount, especially when we showered every Saturday. From start to finish, including stripping and dressing, showering (a solemn affair) was closely supervised by Brother George. We changed into black, loose swimming trunks, the baggier the better, which covered us from above the waist to below the knees.

The shower arrangements were rudimentary but worked without a hitch. Thirty or so boys stood shoulder to shoulder in a narrow trough or channel of water, into which we first threw our stockings. We soaped and scrubbed, and 'marked time' on the stockings at the same time. Overhead, and parallel with the channel, was a long, deep runnel of lukewarm water. When we were well soaped, the Brother pulled a lever which opened small apertures, one over each boy's head, allowing the water to cascade onto him and rinse away the soap. The lever was then pushed home to close the vents and allow the overhead gutter to refill in time for the next batch. Needless to say, the shower room was awash from the stomping of so many feet on the stockings, for which reason we dressed outside in the lower playground, or in a classroom when it rained.

Saturday was also stocking-repair day. Darning our stockings was a skill we learned from each other. Originally a small group, trained to operate knitting machines, 'vamped' the worst of the stockings by knitting new feet on them. The others they darned by hand. But later it was considered unfair that the same group should have to do this all the time, so the Brother ordered every boy to darn his own stockings. We actually enjoyed it and took pride in our darning, competing with each other for neatness. When the stockings were too far gone for hand-darning, the vamping of new feet was contracted to a lady living in the basement flat of 73 Blessington Street in Dublin. I was the boy who delivered the stockings to her (travelling by bus) and collected them a couple of weeks later.

I don't know why I was selected to go to the city for various messages. I met new boys at Kingsbridge station, some of them coming from my old school in Kilkenny, and this even though a boy might have an older brother in Carriglea. I once escorted an older boy to Vaughan's Hotel, Parnell Square, where he was to be interviewed for a job, which he didn't get because the manageress fancied me for the post and tried her best to persuade me to accept it. My poor companion was practically ignored.

Each of the school's two long, open-plan dormitories (there were no cubicles) held about a hundred and fifty beds head to foot in five rows. Central heating was unknown, and I suppose we became used to the cold in winter. A small turf fire at the head of the senior dorm couldn't heat so large a room; nor was it meant to, but it did provide comfort for Brother George as he sat out the hour before lights-out, and afterwards for the night-watchman, who kept it going through the night. The latter sat by the fire and smoked his pipe when he wasn't on rounds of inspection, for at certain times he had to punch special clocks located at strategic places in the institution. The punch mark registered on a paper disc inside each clock, and all the discs were examined the following day by the Brother to confirm that the watchman had been alert and had patrolled the place punctually.

From eight till nine we sat in bed reading library books or the magazine *Our Boys*. At the head of the dormitory was a wireless with an extension to the junior boys' dorm. We enjoyed the wireless on weeknights, but Sunday nights on Radio Athlone were a dead loss. The garda and Columcille céilí bands rotated week about, playing for the Sunday céilí in the Mansion House. Every tune was repeated over and over again for as long as the dance lasted. Some dances were quite long and, essential though the repetition of the music may have been for the céilí dancers at the scene of the broadcast, it was extremely boring for the radio listeners at home. It gave me a dislike of céilí music which has lasted a lifetime. The Brother noticed our boredom, and if he didn't, there were always the brave few who had no qualms about letting him know, in a 'half joking, wholly in earnest' way.

And so it happened that the gramophone pick-up came as an alternative to the wireless. Willie Redmond, the bandmaster, connected the turntable to the back of the wireless set, so there was no necessity to wind it up. When the steel needle lost its sharpness, the sound box gave out a hissing, scraping noise, so a new needle was inserted from a supply in a little tin box like a snuffbox that was kept beside the wireless. We had a few favourite records. Harry Lauder's *Keep Right on to the End of the Road* was Brother George's, but pride of place with us went to Jimmy O'Dea and Harry O'Donovan's comedy sketches: *In the Bookie's Shop*, *At the Abbey Theatre*, *Making a Telephone Call* and *Jimmy O'Dea on the Tram*. We never tired of hearing them. The selection of records was left to Brother George, or Willie Redmond if he was there.

The wireless was more popular than the gramophone, even though broadcasting standards were amateurish compared with those of today. For instance, scheduling of programmes was not the streamlined, precise art it has become, and long delays between programmes were not uncommon. The gaps were filled, believe it or not, by a recording of someone playing on a piano, with one finger, the opening bars of 'O'Donnell Abú'. It was repeated over and over until they were ready with the next programme. It was known as the station's 'identification tune'. Foreign stations had theirs too, and they were a feature of broadcasting later, during the war – the opening bars of the French National Anthem, or of Beethoven's Fifth Symphony (V for victory), for example. Ireland's only sponsored programme then was from the Irish Hospitals Sweepstakes, whose closing motto was ' . . . and so, whether you be on land, on sea, or in the sky, we wish you well, every hour of every day. This is Ian Priestly Mitchell wishing you all a very good night.'

Brother George had a privileged circle of friends in the senior dorm, and in due course I insinuated myself into it, timorously at first to test the waters. We kept him company by the fire. Many's the laugh I gave him without knowing why, and he'd call me his 'philosopher'. It was cosy, comfortable and secure, and I wanted it to last forever. At lights-out the lights were lowered to a rosy glow.

11

News From 'Outside'

Brother Arthur was popular not only among the juniors, because he read to them in the dormitory, but among the seniors as well. When he was in charge of recreation periods, he pasted the daily newspapers to the inside of his classroom window, which overlooked the playground. This kept us abreast of world events, he said. Aviation was front-page news in the early 1930s, when it was commercially in its infancy, and a British newspaper sponsored intercontinental flying races to promote its commercial potential. The long trip from England to Australia was a race that I recall about this time.

Photographs of pioneers of flying, such as Amy Johnson, Amelia Earhart, Colonel Lindbergh, Jim Mollison and our own Colonel Fitzmaurice featured prominently every day. These aviators were household names, heroes and heroines of boys like us, for of course their bravery fired our young imaginations. We jostled for position at the window every morning, eager to read accounts of the previous day's stage of the race. Excitement was high as we scanned the pictures taken at the refuelling stops en route: Southampton, Paris, Marseilles, Rome, Athens and so on. Interest was razor-sharp, for the very idea of flying was hard to grasp. A crowd of eager youngsters teeming around the window, cheering and clapping, was something worth seeing, while Brother Arthur, for the benefit of the boys at the back, read out the report of the previous day's legs. Doubtless history has recorded who won the race I'm speaking of, but it has slipped my mind. I do recall, however, our great disappointment on learning that it was not the Irishman. It consoled us to know that this was due to mechanical failure and not lack of bravery on his part.

In the same way we learned about other major happenings

in the outside world – the kidnapping and murder of Colonel Lindbergh's infant son in America, for instance, and the subsequent trial and execution of one Hauptmann for the crime. A major political crisis in England, referred to by the newspapers as 'the Mrs Simpson affair' was front-page news for a long time also, and came to a head with the abdication of King Edward VIII. We were talking about this, Brother George and I, on the school walk one Sunday. After I had outlined the matter for him, I dismissed it with, 'It seems to me the papers are making an awful fuss about giving up a throne. Sure what can you do with a throne anyway, but sit on it?'

With Brother Arthur we followed the daily progress of the Spanish Civil War. As we saw it, General Franco's 'rebels', as his forces were called, were fighting to free Spain from the evil Communists, whose torture and murder of civilians, including priests and nuns, was often graphically described. Franco was portrayed by the Brother as the great leader of a holy crusade against atheism, so not surprisingly we cheered his successes and prayed for more. The excitement surged whenever Franco captured a major town, and it was explained to us why its capture was crucial to the campaign, and what the developments were likely to be. Years later it was no small surprise to me to learn how unpopular the Franco side was in many western countries, and how some people I admired through their writings (Ernest Hemingway and George Orwell, for instance) had supported the (Communist) Republican side.

Through reading the pasted-up newspapers, we were also brought in touch with events in Abyssinia, now called Ethiopia, after its invasion by Mussolini's armies. Brother Arthur liked to stand among the boys around the display window answering the many questions we had; we saw him as the authority on the world's affairs. We marched around the playground beating a tea chest and singing:

Will you come to Abyssinia, will you come?
Bring your own ammunition and your gun,

Mussolini will be there,
Firing bullets in the air,
Will you come to Abyssinia, will you come?

Events at home also captured our attention. A chap named Edward Ball murdered his mother in Booterstown, not far from us, and as was the custom of the day, the newspaper reports of the trial included lengthy extracts of counsels' cross-examination of witnesses, word for word, so the reader was brought right into the courtroom. We followed this keenly because of its local interest (some of our Sunday walks took us through Booterstown). The trial resulted in a verdict of 'guilty but insane', and Ball was committed to an asylum in Dublin.

Then there was a celebrated custody case for fourteen-year-old Guy Kindersley, son of Lady Oranmore and Browne, of the Guinness family. She won the case. We were amused that the father, a British army officer in India at the time, had declared in an affidavit that he was seeking custody chiefly to save the boy from becoming a 'Sinn Féiner' – or so it was reported.

In October 1936 a major fire occurred in Pearse Street in Dublin, in which three firemen lost their lives. The newspapers showed graphic pictures of the tragic event and the huge public funerals afterwards. There were calls for a public inquiry amid allegations that the firemen had been severely hampered by inadequate water pressure at the scene of the fire. An inquiry was subsequently held, but I don't recall reading about its findings; nor would I learn them until many years had passed. I remember how deeply affected we boys were by the tragedy, and we offered prayers in the chapel for the brave men and their young families. We wrote a school essay about it, and I remember concluding mine with an expression of hope that a suitable monument or plaque would be erected at the site of the fire to honour the victims, so that their heroism would never be forgotten. Which shows how naive I was. Not only was there no memorial, the men's families were shabbily treated by the state.

More than ten years later, I would be passing the site of the fire on my way to work every day, and would look in vain for a memorial. Only the boarded-up ruins of the buildings stood gaping at the sky, a mute reminder to a heartless city whose legislators preferred to name new roads and apartment blocks after themselves. Today not even the ruins remain.

More than thirty years after that time, while I was out walking with my family in Limerick city, I met Brother Arthur again. He was over eighty then, and was far from the stalwart I had known, yet I had no difficulty recognising him. I was reluctant to accost him, thinking he wouldn't know me after so many years. Yet I didn't want our chance meeting to pass without a word, so I opened with a hesitant 'Excuse me, Brother Arthur, you won't remember me of course – '

'Why do you assume I don't remember you?' he asked, with that twinkle in his eye that brought me back many years. 'Of course I do. Who could ever forget Joe Dunne?' I wondered if he meant it as a compliment, but his impish smile reassured me. I was impressed and flattered by his feat of memory, because I had never been a pupil in his class and had considered myself, at best, on the fringes of his acquaintance when at school. Besides, I was one of who knows how many boys he had known, in various schools, in a long career as a teacher. Thousands, probably. Further, I could think of no reason why I should be remembered.

He was living in retirement in Limerick, and with boyish enthusiasm he told me how he loved to travel often to Shannon Airport to see the huge jet planes. This was so typical of the man I had known long ago. I gave him my address and invited him to visit on the following weekend. He must have told his confrères about me, for sadly, I received word a few days later that he had passed away in his sleep. I was stunned, and have often wondered about the extraordinary coincidence of our chance meeting, days before his death. Only then I learned that his name was Charles Firmin Arthur; we had always assumed that Arthur was his Christian name.

Besides the Brothers, there were a few lay teachers, the most notable being Mr Lavelle, known as the Master. He was burly, over six feet tall, and with the build of a policeman, square-headed and bull-necked. These features, combined with his reputation, made him feared on sight, and no newcomer was left long in being told how 'hard' the Master was. One of the first things he heard was, 'Wait till you get to the Master's class . . . Ooh!' – his fate being left suspended, too horrible for words. The Master taught the senior class, and since to a schoolboy one year is a long time, and three or four a lifetime, we would say confidently, 'He's an old man now – must be fifty at least – and please God he'll be dead an' gone before we join the senior class.'

He cycled each morning from Dún Laoghaire, and stayed until teatime or later, for he also supervised our play periods from time to time. He would find some reason to suspend our recreation; any excuse would do. For instance, he made us form into lines for Swedish drill, boringly jerking our arms up and down, each movement repeated ad nauseam to the blow of his whistle till we were on the point of dropping. Or he ordered us down to the farm for 'ten minutes' of back-breaking work weeding the crops or harvesting potatoes. One boy had the misfortune to be overheard saying under his breath: 'I know the Master's "ten minutes" – two hours.' For that he was severely slapped with the stick, which was like the leg of a chair.

As he used the stick for the slightest cause, the Master was expert at whacking it right on target – the extreme tips of the fingers. Should a boy be foolish enough to move his hand slightly in hope of causing the Master to miss, he would get double measure. Unerringly the stick landed with full force every time, the pain shooting up the arm to the shoulder and lasting some time after, for the Master was no weakling. It was excruciating, especially when, on occasion, the swelling and soreness of the fingers had not had time to abate since a previous slapping. The Master was the fly in the ointment, the serpent in the Garden of Eden, and had he not been there my years in

Carriglea would have been perfect bliss. However, until I had to join his class – oh unhappy day – I would have to stay out of his way.

For potato-picking on the farm we spread out at arms' length in a single line the entire length of the fields, and when the horse-drawn plough passed us by, a rich crop of potatoes was unearthed at our feet. We put them in wooden boxes evenly placed along the line, a back-breaking job. The farm boys took them away to prepared sites, where they built potato mounds four or five feet high, and some six feet long. They covered the mounds with alternate layers of potato-stalks and earth as protection against the winter weather. From there they were collected in instalments for the future dinners of some three hundred boys plus staff; when I say that we had potatoes for dinner six days a week all year round, you have an idea how big the harvest was.

There were a few glass presses or cabinets full of books in the Master's classroom, and Willie Redmond, the bandmaster, decided to index the books and establish a school lending library. I was delighted to be included among the helpers, because I was fond of reading. Incidentally, when I left school I was quite surprised to discover that the system in use in the public libraries in Dublin was the same as that which we thought we had designed in school. There were marvellous books in our library, and I can still recall my enjoyment on first reading *The Forge of Clohogue, My New Curate, Glenanaar, A Lad of the O'Friels* and *Lost on Dubh Corrig*. I told the stories to my companions on many a Sunday walk. My favourite reading time was in bed, an hour before lights-out, with the gramophone or wireless in the background.

A close watch was kept on reading matter that came to the school via the boys' relatives. For some reason comics were banned – we never knew why – and visitors were informed of this at the start. New books had to be handed up to be censored by Brother George, who always smiled when asked to 'censure this book please'. It was only a formality because I never knew a book to be confiscated, apart from the occasional comic book which a lad might chance his arm with.

A monthly magazine called *Our Boys* was published by the Christian Brothers in the city, and our school got a couple of dozen copies. They were distributed in alphabetical order of our names, and were avidly read and passed around. *Our Boys* contained everything a boy would want to read – lots of adventure stories, a mystery or two, and a gripping ghost story told by 'Kitty the Hare, the Travelling Woman of Munster', which was written by Victor O'Dea Power. There were also items of interest for your scrapbook, headed 'Scissors and Paste', and a jokes page bearing the legend: 'A little laughter now and then is relished by the wisest men.' A prize of half a crown went to the sender of the best joke (and boy did the editor get some corny ones!) What amused us more than the jokes themselves was the fact that readers were urged by the editor to write the word 'JOKE' clearly in the top left-hand corner of the envelope when posting them in. 'Otherwise,' we laughed, 'he won't know what it is.'

We were taught to respect books – all books, not only those from the library – and you'd 'feel the leather' if you were caught mistreating them. That included dog-earing the pages, or stiffening your collar between the pages and putting the book under your pillow. The latter, we were told, 'damaged the book's binding'. It mattered not whether the book was your own property or the school's, you'd be punished nevertheless.

12

THE BAND AND THE SHOP

The bandmaster was Willie Redmond. In his mid-twenties, he was a past pupil of the school, which probably explains why we referred to him by his first name, although we respectfully called him 'Sir' in his presence. A short time after I came to Carriglea, he sent for me and, guessing the reason, I ran to the band room in great excitement. He asked me to smile and show my teeth, then, taking a spare instrument from the cabinet, he said, 'Here you are, Joe, this is a B-flat clarinet. I'm going to teach you how to play it. Are you prepared to work hard, though?'

'Yes sir.'

'Well if you are, you'll play in the band some day, if you're good enough.'

I promised to do my very best. I was thrilled; I'd have promised anything.

His sharp features and thick spectacles gave him a severe, crotchety look, but he never carried a strap or stick, except the featherweight baton he used for conducting the band. Nor did I ever see him give anyone a slap. He was, however, short on patience, and lost his temper and shouted when he heard a wrong note. You never saw anyone so annoyed for so little cause – a B flat blown instead of a B natural, for instance. His face flushed scarlet, he struck the music stand with his baton, often breaking it, and we younger ones cowered in fear. But in time we got used to it because it happened so often, wrong notes being by no means a rarity in those parts. At other times he just bawled at us at the top of his voice – he had to shout to be heard above all the instruments playing together. His acute hearing was legendary: he could detect a wrong note even down in the nether regions of sound in the back row of basses and trombones, and this while the band was playing full blast in the enclosed space of the small room. He was a perfectionist, and the band had to produce the sound and precision that he wanted – nothing else would do. He had a job getting what he wanted, and for that reason appeared always to be in bad humour. He could play all the instruments himself, which he demonstrated when necessary by taking from its player any instrument – oboe, clarinet, flute, cornet, horn, trombone or bass – to show how a particular passage should be played.

The band room was on the ground floor at the rear, form-ing the corner between the east and south wings. It had a stone floor and a tiny fireplace, and was barely big enough for the band of about thirty, plus a dozen or so learners (there had to be a number of reserves to fill vacancies, which arose about three or four times a year).

Joe White was a beginner on the E-flat clarinet, a smaller version of my B-flat one, and we helped each other to learn. From Willie Redmond we learned how to read music, and from members of the band we learned the fingering and blowing techniques. We practised two hours a day in the same room with the band members, everyone playing his own exercise – a variety of tunes and scales, in different keys – and all as loud as we could; the noise was almost deafening. I found the clarinet too heavy to hold for so long every day, and after a few weeks my right thumb, which bore the weight, became very painful and swollen. I was switched to the oboe, a lighter instrument. Its tone was lighter too, so I had to blow the oboe with its bell held against my music, that I might hear its thin, feeble sound bounced back to me over the din.

The oboe player in the band was my monitor, John Keogh, whose job it was to teach me. He was a good player himself and a fine lad, the sort we juniors looked up to with respect. There were many like him, their character and personal development polished to a degree that would fit them for the outside world they would shortly face, often on their own. Under John's tuition I soon became good enough to play second oboe by his side in the band, and later to take his place when he left for good. The band's repertoire was large and varied: *The Bohemian Girl, The Quaker Girl, Carmen, Faust* and *Manon,* and, of course, Gilbert and Sullivan too; most of the popular overtures; and not forgetting countless arrangements of Irish airs. Then there were the marches (probably acquired from British army bands): 'The Great Little Army', 'Colonel Bogey', 'The Middy', 'Old Comrades' and 'On the Quarter Deck'. There were also marches with flavours of British India, such as 'The Punjab'. I remember snatches of these marches still, although they are rarely heard nowadays – at least, on this side of the Irish Sea.

When selections of old popular tunes such as *Songs from the Gay Nineties* and *Fifty Years of Song* were purchased, the bandmaster deleted all the lyrics. He did this by typing the letter 'X' through every letter, so that the words could not be read, however hard we tried. Of course, we came to know the words when we left school, because the songs, all music-hall smash hits in their day, retained their popularity, and were still sung at parties and hooleys in the 1940s.

The reason for the censorship was that the lyrics had a love motif, quite innocuous, but nevertheless the boys had to be protected from anything of that kind. For the word 'love' was strictly taboo in the school, except in prayer, or in reference to something inanimate. For example, a popular song of the day was 'Ol' Faithful', which Willie Redmond taught us for a variety show he produced in the school hall. A cowboy sang to his horse, 'Ol' Faithful, we roam the range together . . . ', and one of the lines went: 'Carry me home to the *one* I love'. That had to be cleaned up for us, so it was changed to 'Carry me back to the *home* I love'. No wonder we left school believing love to be a dirty word – improper and sinful.

There were frequent band engagements, especially in the summer; I can hardly describe how excited we were before them. First, everybody, even the woodwind, had to polish the brass instruments – no easy task, because of their winding tubing. It was messy, too, but we did it with happy anticipation. The smell of Brasso has brought pleasant memories ever since. Next, we cleaned ourselves, polished our boots, put on our Sunday clothes (for we didn't have a band uniform), brilliantined and combed our hair, and were ready to go. Each band boy was responsible for seeing that his instrument, band parts, music stand, lyre and other accessories were packed in one of two large wooden chests, then off with us in a hired bus, singing for joy. Somehow, as I remember it, the sun always shone those days.

Every Sunday in May we played at the Marian devotions, walking in a long weaving procession in the grounds of the Oblates in Inchicore or Mount Argus monastery in Harold's Cross. The 'May Processions', as they were called, were extremely popular, and attracted people in their thousands from all over the city. Afterwards, in the space in front of the church, we played musical selections for the crowd. During my silent passages, or 'bars' rest', I scanned the faces for my mother, who always managed to come, and when the recital was over we would have a stealthy cuddle. I often thought of that day, years before, when, at that very venue, a four-year-old boy had prophesied with envy that one day he would be playing in such a band.

After packing away our instruments and other bits and pieces, we were shown to the refectory for tea, bread and jam. We sat at a long table, the bandmaster and Father Superior at the end of the room, at right angles to us. The priests, guessing correctly what a treat it was for us, kept the jam-covered bread coming in an unbroken chain of supply to our tables. Those in the kitchen must have been hard pressed indeed in coping with the demand. All the while we were keeping a wary eye on the bandmaster, hoping he was too engrossed to notice how much we were eating.

Dún Laoghaire was the last bastion of the old order. 'Kingstown', they persisted in calling it, in commemoration of a royal visit to Ireland years before. Our band was once engaged to play musical selections at a private garden fête given by a person who must have been a member of the former establishment. A lot of important people attended, including the Lord Mayor of

Dublin, Alderman Alfie Byrne. The gentlemen, in formal wear, including silk top hats, stood around in small groups with drinks in their hands, chatting importantly. The ladies sat at white circular tables, sipped tea genteelly and wore wide-rimmed picture hats which were popular among the upper classes at that time. The setting was great – magnificent green lawns and colourful flower beds shown to perfection in bright warm sunshine. For all the attention paid to the band, however, we might as well have been on the moon. And yet the bandmaster was asked by a fussy body in charge what item we intended playing next. On being told it was called 'God Save Ireland, Cried the Heroes', the man said alarmingly that he couldn't have that – oh no, that wouldn't do at all. 'Haven't you something more suitable? Anything but that!'

'Certainly,' the bandmaster replied. 'How about "Tramp, Tramp, Tramp, the Boys Are Marching?"'

'Splendid,' said the man, much relieved, obviously unaware that the two songs had the same melody – it was the words that were different.

The band occasionally marched through the town, drawing crowds of people who inevitably fell in behind it. We would be greeting people like Cardinal McRory, Archbishop of Armagh, disembarking from the mailboat on his return from Rome. There was always a huge crowd. Once we played at the North Wall in Dublin for the cardinal and the Irish pilgrimage to Lourdes before they boarded the liner *Athenia*. The pilgrimage was a very important event in those days, and a huge crowd attended to give it a send-off, including Alfie Byrne, whose waxed moustache, bowler hat, butterfly collar, and gold watch-chain singled him out from the crowd, even though he was smaller than average in height. The event was broadcast by Radio Athlone, as RTÉ was known then, and we were thrilled to realise that our band was being heard all over the country on the wireless. What a tragedy occurred a few years later, in the early stages of the war, when that beautiful ship was torpedoed and sunk by Germany with heavy loss of life.

Our band also attended annual drill displays mounted by boys from O'Connell's and Westland Row Christian Brothers' schools. The boys performed the drill movements in time to waltz medleys like 'Gold and Silver' and 'The Blue Danube'. Microphones carried our music to the far ends of the grounds. Hundreds of boys in white suits performed figure-marching and we blared out 'O'Donnell Abú' and 'The Minstrel Boy' when they marched on and off the grounds. They made a wonderful sight, drilling and marching with perfect precision. Strange to say, we were never engaged to play in Croke Park, Ireland's prestigious sport's stadium. That privilege went to Artane Boys' Band, because Artane School, also run by the Christian Brothers, was a far larger institution than ours (its pupil capacity was three times greater). Probably because of that, the Artane Boys' Band enjoyed a wider reputation and was more popular, especially in the city, whereas Carriglea Boys' Band and school were hardly known outside Dún Laoghaire, Blackrock and Monkstown.

Some boys seemed always to have money to spend, because their people were regular visitors. To facilitate them, sweets were sold once a week from boxes laid out on a windowsill in the main playground. NKM toffees, aniseed balls and bulls'-eyes were the most popular, at ten or twelve a penny. For those who wanted to show off and splash out, there were slabs of Mickey Mouse toffee at the luxury price of fivepence. I ran the shop. My commission was a penny in the shilling, but I had to wait for it until the box was sold out. The toffee bars took ages to sell, nobody wanting to spend fivepence in one go.

To replenish my stocks, I walked to the wholesalers in Dún Laoghaire. There was a constant demand for personal things and 'extras' for tea, and I had permission to purchase them. I went to Woolworth's in Lower George's Street, where one could buy practically anything. The most common needs were: boys' ties at threepence; Wren and Cherry Blossom boot polish at three ha'pence; collar studs at a penny a pair (front and back); brilliantine hair oil, twopence a phial; torch batteries and bulbs; and bootlaces, hair combs and so on. No list was complete with-

Carriglea Park School Band, Dún Laoghaire (1936)
The author is second from the right in the front row

out Oxo beef cubes and Lucknow Sauce, while thick doorsteps of ginger cake at a penny were all the rage too. I was trying to save for a pocket watch promised by Paddy Carr for half a crown, but thanks to the same perishing ginger cake, it took well over a year to save the thirty pence.

I had a disaster, however, and nearly lost the shop because I accepted from the wholesaler a box of conversation lozenges, so called because each sweet had some motif inscribed on it. Naturally I hadn't seen those sweets before, and I took them solely on the wholesaler's recommendation. I displayed the boxes on a window ledge in the playground and was ready for my first sale of the day when Brother George happened along.

'Well Joe, and what have you got there – the usual, I suppose?' he said pleasantly.

I named each item and then proudly showed off my initiative in departing from the normal stock. Introducing the conversation lozenges, I said proudly, borrowing the wholesaler's jargon, 'Sir, this is a new line. The wholesaler said they'll be a real money-spinner *and* they're only twelve a penny.' This was compared with others at ten and eight a penny.

He picked up a few sweets and read their mottos, then read some more, and more, his breathing quickening and rising in a crescendo the more he read, his hair falling down over his forehead, his face reddening, his lips pursing – all the well-known warning signals were flashing good-oh that something terrible was wrong, but what could it be? 'Better interrupt his reading before he explodes,' I said to myself.

'Ahem, is there something wrong, sir?'

He didn't answer for a long minute but continued reading the sweets' motifs.

'If only he'd stop readin',' I thought. 'He's only getting madder.'

At last he turned to me, scarlet with rage, and as if by magic a hush descended on the boys nearby and began to spread across the yard, heralding a major event. I had seen this happen before. It was as if an electrical discharge was emitted by the Brother as soon as the hand on his humour gauge reached the red. Snatching up the offending sweets, he fumed, 'In future you'll stick to the approved items and never *ever* go outside them again. Do I make myself clear?'

The whole playground was quiet now and he had no need to shout.

'Yes sir, but – '

'In fact, from now on you'll show me your list before you go to the wholesaler. Understand?'

'Yes sir, I'm very sorry, sir. But the wholesaler said – '

'"The wholesaler said",' he mimicked. 'Any man with half an eye can see you're a fool in matters like this.'

'Yes sir, but I'd no idea – '

'That's it in a nutshell: you've no idea. Lucky for you I see that you acted out of blind ignorance and stupidity.'

I didn't mention anything to the wholesaler afterwards, not wanting her to know that there had been trouble, so when she asked me how the new sweets went down I told her they weren't sold yet, which was no lie. And then the way out came to me: in a few weeks' time, on my three-day Christmas holidays, I would buy some of the offensive sweets and see for myself.

And so it happened that in due course I stood in Mrs O'Flanagan's shop in James' Street, Dublin, timidly asking if I could have a penn'orth of conversation lozenges please. I waited nervously, embarrassed, as though I was buying a bad book or something, and I actually looked over my shoulder in case the ubiquitous Brother happened along. Mrs O'Flanagan took ages reaching for the jar of sweets and prising off the lid. While doing so she joked with me. 'You know, you're the first kid in a long time to ask for these correctly,' she said. 'You'd want to hear some of the names they have – "corporation lossingers" and even "constipation lossingers".' She screwed a piece of newspaper into a cone shape and counted a dozen of the sweets into it. I was wishing madly for her to hurry up, not because I was impatient to learn their secret, but because I was so tense and apprehensive. I couldn't be sure that the Brother wasn't in some way aware of my crime and was all set to appear on the scene at that very moment. Indeed, had he done so it would not have surprised me in the least, for his apparent ability to be in two places at once had been demonstrated many times before.

On leaving school in a year's time, I would meet Mrs O'Flanagan again. She would become a second mother to me and would treat me as a member of her family. She had six children, and indeed no one would be surprised when, in the fullness of time, I would marry Agnes, one of her daughters.

Still shaking from nerves, and full of guilt, I inched out of the shop and crossed the street into quieter Basin Lane before unfolding the wrapping, safe from the eyes of passers-by. The blood rushed in gallons to my face as I read 'Kiss me quick', 'I love you', 'Will you be mine?', 'I'm mad about you', 'Are you doing anything tonight?' and 'You are my true love' on the heart-shaped lozenges. At last I understood and appreciated the close call I had had in not having sold some of the sweets. Knowing as I did my school's attitude towards 'love' (or anything to do with it), had any of the sweets circulated among the boys, there would have been holy murder.

13

MIXED FRUIT AND THE MATRON

The middle of September saw preparations for the annual blackberry-picking. We made 'mashers' from spent spools obtained from the tailors' shop; into each spool we stuck a piece of stick or pencil to serve as a handle. Then we got hold of jam jars, from where I can't remember; they appeared on the scene when needed. Every boy managed to get one, and round its neck he tied a piece of string as a handle to hold it by. Away we went in double file, under Brother George's supervision, to scramble excitedly over the blind side of Killiney Hill, about five miles away, and on the slopes of which grew a profusion of the most luscious blackberries you ever saw.

As we picked, we pressed them into a pulpy mash we called 'jam'. The harder we mashed, the more berries we had room for – two into the jar, one into the mouth. After an hour or so we turned for home, walking in pairs, mashing and licking. When we reached the village of Kill o' the Grange, close by the school, a halt was called by whistle to allow those with the money (three ha'pence) to buy half a pound of brown sugar in the small shop. Brown sugar, not white, was best for making jam, we had heard. If you hadn't the money itself it didn't matter; you would get a fistful from someone who had. The donors poured it into eager hands – hands that were far from clean, having been rooting the previous hour in and under the bushes. We gave not a thought to niceties such as hygiene: that never bothered us. We happily mixed our share of sugar into the mess to heighten the illusion of jam and we relished it, offering a lick of the masher to friends and tasting theirs in return. Spreading it onto our tea-time bread was not to be considered – we got beef dripping for that – and not until several days after our 'jam' was consumed direct from the jars did our fingers and mouths regain their normal colour.

The most memorable blackberry-picking year for me was the one in which I unwittingly became involved in a raid on an orchard. Four or five lads stumbled across a clump of crab-apple trees in a quiet copse hidden on the hillside. At least they must have been crab-apple trees, for they appeared to be growing wild, and the absence of a wall or fence led us to believe that they were on public property, or no man's land. The lads had 'found an orchard', they said, with jubilant squeals, and quickly they attacked the task of picking apples to mix with the blackberries.

Instinct told me they would get into trouble – not for taking the 'crabbers', but for being apart from the main body of boys without permission. I became concerned that they'd be caught, and from outside the copse in loud urgent whispers I called again and again for the invisible raiders to come out.

Unfortunately, some boy snitched to Brother George, and in the telling I must have been described as the lookout. Our blackberries were confiscated, and in school we got a public 'telling off' and six painful slaps of the leather on each hand before being sent to bed without our tea. My plea of being only an innocent bystander was not accepted – in fact, I thought my slaps were harder than those the others got because I was the only one who denied being involved. It was the injustice of being accused in the wrong that hurt me more than the punishment itself, and I have never forgotten it on that account. However, that was not the worst of the affair by any means.

There was a great hullabaloo about it, and of course it came to the ears of the Master, in whose class it was our misfortune to be that year. 'Any boy who commits an offence outside the precincts of the school,' he thundered, 'brings down shame and dishonour on the whole school!' He thought we had been let off too lightly, and ordered that in future the boys involved in 'the shameful incident' should shout 'Mixed fruit!' whenever we were up for punishment for wrongdoing, or failure at lessons. It automatically doubled the punishment. That didn't simply mean double the number of slaps; it meant getting the second part of the punishment on the other hand. As I was right-handed, my left was far more sensitive to pain. It was a matter of honour not to flinch in front of one's classmates, and with a façade of bravery, but trembling inside in craven terror, I offered my hand palm upwards, as high as I hoped to get away with to shorten the downward swipe. But to frustrate that, and to guide his aim, the Master pressed my hand down with the stick (he was far too wily) before smashing it onto the target, again and again.

Unerringly the stick cracked the tips of my fingers, sending through me, like electric shocks, agonies of burning, stinging pain. After each slap I silently invoked a heartfelt prayer that it would be the last, but in fact the uncertainty of the number was part of the agony.

As if that were not bad enough, the injustice of my being grouped with the 'mixed fruit' boys was aggravated when I was punished for petty mistakes the Master ignored in others in the class. The punishments went far beyond the bounds of reason-ableness, and followed so closely upon each other that I was unable to hold my instrument at band practice.

When a Brother 'told you off', especially Brother George, and rarer still when he slapped you, what you felt more than the pain was the loss of his favour, friendship and good grace. Not so the Master. With him it was physical only, without emotion, unless your hatred of him counted. In fact the more he slapped the more he enjoyed it, to judge by his smile. He was a sadist. It is hard to estimate now how long the 'mixed fruit' episode lasted; certainly it was many weeks. At first our shouts of 'mixed fruit' caused sniggers among some in the class, but soon the un-fairness of the situation was apparent even to the dumbest, and everyone looked on in sympathetic silence. As I had done so often in the past, I resorted to praying to God for help and pro-tection. When the other lads involved asked me to be spokes-man, I agreed, even though I looked on them as the authors of my misfortune. My nerve failed, however, when I approached the Brother, and the tears came. I found myself making my own case only – i.e., stressing my complete innocence in the apple affair, and ignoring the involvement of the other boys. 'We've been over that ground before,' he said dismissively. 'Why you continue to whinge about something that's long past and done with, I do not know.'

'But sir, it isn't finished at all,' I protested, and went on to tell of all that we had suffered since.

'What! After all this time?'

'Yes, sir.'

His face took on that certain look. There was no mistaking its meaning: it was a sight not often seen, but when it was, we were in no doubt about the fury behind it. With flushed face and hair falling down over his forehead (a sure sign of his wrath), he questioned me at length. Several others were summoned for questioning later, including some in the 'mixed fruit' group. I don't know what took place afterwards between the two men, and I am glad I didn't witness their meeting, but it brought the 'mixed fruit' episode to an end. Nor was there any repercussion from the Master, which had been my chief worry about going over his head.

Like Miss O'Reilly in Kilkenny, the Master taught his class by pain and fear of pain. We learned everything by rote, repeating aloud in singing monotone or silently, our fingers in our ears. We learned every subject 'off by heart': money tables, history (dates, battles, people), the rules of Irish and English grammar, and geography (rivers, capes, mountain ranges, European capitals, chief towns and principal products). While we were thus engrossed, he walked slowly around the room, now and then pausing to look out the window, his back to the class, as he surreptitiously took a pinch of snuff. He would round suddenly on some boy at random to 'hear' the lesson, and any sign of hesitation or stumbling in the recital earned for the unfortunate boy several severe slaps of the stick on the tips of his fingers. The Master's cruel appetite would be sated for the moment.

The fear in the classroom was palpable. You could smell it, and you might even catch it from an ashen-faced classmate whose eye you chanced to meet at the wrong moment, for it was contagious. From what I heard in later life, practically every school in the country had at least one teacher like the Master, who believed that fear and pain were the best vehicles for conveying knowledge. Until it was outlawed in 1982, corporal punishment was legally practised in all schools, public and private, primary and secondary. So much has today's society turned against it that this treatment is now termed 'child abuse'. Yet for decades it was a daily feature of life in schools throughout the land, with the knowledge of the government, the blessing of the Church, and the approval of the public at large.

I was never more devout in my prayers than in 1936, the year I spent in the Master's class. So frequently did I call on divine assistance to evade his personal attentions that, had I chanced by some accident to die, I should have been whisked at once straight to heaven. And yet, in spite of everything, his teaching methods worked for me, because after a while I became well versed in all subjects – except perhaps maths, which was to cause me problems for a while yet. The result was that I had little to fear outside maths hour, and so gradually drifted into calmer waters.

Brother George was extremely generous, and often ordered crates of apples or oranges for the school, and even large Spanish onions, mild enough to eat as you would an apple. Damsons were also a great treat. Once he bought enough damsons to have jam made in such quantities that we had it for tea every Friday for about four months. There were, of course, the few boys who didn't like it, and sneeringly called it 'gravel jam' because of all the stones it contained. There is no pleasing some people.

Once Nurse Scanlon, the matron, made vegetable marrow and ginger jam for the Brothers, and when news of that got around someone spread a false rumour that she had laced the jam with a laxative. To nobody's surprise, except perhaps the matron's, the jam was offloaded onto the boys. I was lucky enough to get a couple of jars of it. It was delicious, and I must say that I haven't tasted the equal of it to this day.

Everybody liked Nurse Scanlon, even though behind her

back we called her 'the oul' wan'. Middle-aged, tall and built like an opera singer, she was my idea of a lady. Most of her time was spent making jam, or rhubarb wine, or fireside rugs. I was once numbered among a few boys she roped in to make a large, plain fireside rug. Having shown us what to do, she left us to it. At the rate of an hour or so a day, it took several weeks to complete, all of us sitting on two beds in the infirmary, the rug canvas spread on a table between us. As a reward we were to have a 'high tea', for which she invited us to set our own menu. I included 'a glass of Matron's famous rhubarb wine' in the suggested fare, but there was nothing doing! The tea was a great success even so.

Every boy in the school was robust and healthy, so she had an easy time of it as far as her nursing duties were concerned. I don't remember seeing a sick boy in one of the infirmary's few beds. An occasional scraped knee or stubbed toe in summer (when we played in bare feet) hardly taxed Matron's nursing skills. Treatment was always the same: a daub of iodine, and maybe a small bandage or sticking plaster. In her eyes iodine was a cure-all. Bottles stood in rows on the shelves, and the infirmary reeked of it – in fact, if the wind blew from that quarter, you could smell iodine a couple of hundred yards away. Boys with sore throats and chest colds in winter had their fronts liberally painted for days, until their skin began to flake, and they got a hard time from classmates who objected to sitting near them.

To Matron perhaps belongs the chief credit for our robust health. From time to time she ordered us to assemble in the playground to receive a small amount of lukewarm water in a mug, and under her supervision sedlitz powders were distributed in two small paper packets: a blue one containing a laxative powder which we stirred into the water, and a white one. When the contents of the latter were added, the mixture fizzed and sparkled as we drank it down. Also, once or twice in winter, we had to line up in the playground for a tablespoon of cod-liver oil, which was heartily detested to a man, because it kept coming back in our throats for the rest of the day. If anyone made a fuss about taking it, however, he was given a second dose.

One winter there was an outbreak of flu, and about a hundred boys were affected – or claimed to be. They were ordered to bed in the senior dormitory, but boredom soon exposed the majority as fakes and they claimed a miraculous cure after the first day. However, they were made to stick it out for a week, by which time they were truly sick of cod-liver oil. Neither the Matron nor Brother George had been taken in; in fact they were highly amused. The rest of us enjoyed it too, since normal class studies were suspended for the week.

Only rarely was a boy ill enough for Doctor Frost to be called from Dún Laoghaire. The presence outside the infirmary of his shiny red Morris motor car with its chrome grille and bumpers attracted a crowd. Once a boy had a tooth extracted in the town and a bad infection set in, distorting his face to twice its normal size. He was rushed to St Michael's Hospital in the doctor's car, and thereafter the school went to the dental hospital in Lincoln Place in Dublin for our dental needs. For some reason I was detailed to escort the three or four boys at a time on those visits.

Matron was patriotic through and through, and at the drop of a hat would talk about the 1916 Rising, the Troubles and the Truce. Years later I learned that she had been a close friend of Thomas Ashe, who had played an active part in the Rising and who died afterwards on hunger strike. It was said that he and Matron were engaged to be married.

Being the only female among hundreds of males in the school (apart from seldom-seen Cook, and Rose, the Brothers' ancient parlour maid) and given the undemanding nature of her duties, Matron must have been very lonely for female company. Her only visitor was Mrs Tom Clarke, widow of one of the executed leaders of the 1916 Rising, and since she was involved in politics and hadn't much time to spare, she didn't visit very often.

Matron once selected me for a special treat – a visit to the cinema, my first ever. While we waited at Dean's Grange Cross for the Dublin United Tramway Company bus – all buses were single-decker then – she said, 'We'll sit in the front seat when it comes and make believe we're in our own private car.' She took me to the Capitol Theatre to see a talking picture, *A Tale of Two Cities*, starring Ronald Colman. Nearly weak from excitement, I looked around in open-mouthed wonder at the theatre's sumptuous fitments: gilt walls, ornate ceiling and fancy lights. It was what I imagined a palace to be. I wallowed in the plush velvet seat, the like of which I had never seen before. I could hardly contain my excitement, and asked Matron what was going to happen and how did the 'pictures' work. Even as she returned a non-committal 'Wait and see', the lights dimmed and the curtains opened to reveal a screen which lit up with a trailer of a coming musical called *Rose Marie*, starring Nelson Eddie and Jeannette MacDonald. I couldn't believe what I was seeing – and hearing. It was a miracle.

Presently, the main film started. I had no idea what it would be about, never having read the book, for, strange to say, our library had none of Dickens' works, although some extracts appeared in our English reader. Consequently, I was totally unprepared for what followed: the whole concept of moving, talking pictures was new to me. Some scenes of the Terror were grim, frightening and extremely gruesome, and I trembled. I was a participant in the events, yet aware at the same time that they belonged to the past. The cinema was a huge time machine which had whisked me back in history to the French Revolution, so that when the film came to an end I was breathless and tired, as though just back from a journey in time.

We stood outside the Capitol Theatre, Matron and I, back in the present again, and as she took my arm to head for home, she felt me trembling and noticed my agitation. We returned inside to the cinema's restaurant where, over a cup of bittersweet tea, she put me at ease. Everything was performed by actors, and no one had been killed or even hurt. 'Actors are wonderful people,' she said, 'they can make anything appear to happen. Anything.' This amazed me so much that there and then I re-

115

solved to become an actor when I left school. This, my first visit to the cinema, was the biggest excitement of my life and gave me something to tell my companions on Sunday walks for a long time. I don't think I thanked Matron enough for her kindness, and I'm sorry to say that when I eventually came to leave school it didn't occur to me to say goodbye to her. That is something I regret to this day.

Some time afterwards the whole school were taken in special buses to the Savoy Cinema in Dublin to see *The Charge of the Light Brigade*, starring Errol Flynn, and featuring dashing cavalry in red and white uniforms, gold braid and brass helmets. In the interval Philip Dore ascended spooklike from a hole in the floor, playing an organ. Six months after that we had a similar treat, when we were taken to see Spencer Tracy in *Captains Courageous*. We had a special interest in this because it also starred a boy our own age named Freddie Bartholomew.

14

GAMES AND SPORTS

We played a variety of games during recreation hours. Handball was the main one because it was played all year round, unlike the others, which came and went with their respective 'seasons'. There was a double handball alley in the upper yard, and it was a pity the game was not organised officially, because some players were highly skilled, their skill wasted in aimless play. The spice of competition would have sharpened that skill no end and heightened interest in the game as well. To see the top-class players in action was a sight worth witnessing. For ordinary players like me, the big drawback attached to getting a game was that whether one played or not depended on one's popularity rating with the owner of a ball – that and his humour at the time.

The better players used 'Elephant Standard' handballs from Elvery's of Dublin, but only a few could afford them. The others scraped a tennis ball against the wall to remove the 'fluff' or coating of wool from it, which improved its bounce a little. Where handball was concerned, one way or another (playing or merely watching) excitement was assured. Scraped knuckles was one of the commonest causes of visits to the infirmary, the injury acquired through trying to strike the ball when it was too close to the side wall. A dab of iodine and maybe a sticking plaster, and back he came to the game.

As far as I could make out, the 'seasons' which controlled the other games came and went with the wave of a magic wand. For instance, in late August a large number of old worn motor tyres were taken out of storage. This was an assortment of tyres from different makes of cars and lorries. Every boy selected one and ran around the playground beating it with hand or stick to keep it upright and rolling. The tyres were our chief playthings in early autumn, but after five or six weeks, more or less by general consent, they were put away for another year, someone having decided they had gone 'out of season'. It was remarkable. A favourite game with the tyres was to roll one as fast as possible the length of the playground without having it knocked down by an opponent's tyre wheeled against it with force. We picked teams for this, and should you be unlucky enough to have Ape for an opponent you had no chance of making it successfully, for he had a deadly aim, and could whip a heavy lorry tyre up to a tremendous speed with no apparent effort. He stood head and shoulders over his own age group, and was noted (and respected) for his strength. Another huge boy was called Zulu. Ape and Zulu were the giants of the school. They were called upon whenever heavy articles needed lifting or shifting, and they were glad of the chance to display their strength. Once, one of the trees that skirted the football field was blown down in a storm. We were treated to the sight of the two boys dismembering it with saw and axe, roots and all, and physically hoisting the heavy timber onto a dray to be carted away. Years later I was surprised to see a crane being employed to do work which the boys would have done without effort.

Other seasonal playthings were cigarette cards, which came our way via the boys' relatives on visiting day. Hours were spent flipping a card over and over in the air, and bets were laid, with cards as stakes, on whether it would come to rest picture-side or 'blank'-side up. Your stock of cards grew or dwindled depending on how skilful your opponent was in getting his 'flipper' to land to suit him. Or you pasted two cards together to produce a 'stiffer', which you shied towards the wall with the object of getting it to land closer to the wall than your opponent's.

Marbles also appeared seasonally and there was a variety of games to be played with them, all with side bets, using marbles as stakes, the most skilful players scooping their opponents' marbles. When the season came to an abrupt end, however, the winners finished with pockets full of marbles and no one to play with them. From then until the season opened again, they were worthless. No one knew why a season began when it did, or who determined its length. Strangely, its start and finish were accepted by all without challenge.

In addition to the upper and lower playgrounds, a large recreation hall was available for play in wet weather. Its wooden floor was well worn by generations of boys' hobnailed boots, except for hard knots which protruded. These hurt the feet in summer when we played barefoot or in light sandals. Consequently, games in the hall were of a sedentary kind – cards and jack-stones. A large stage fitted with wings and curtains accommodated plays and musical revues, usually produced by Willie Redmond, although Brother Comerford produced *Iosagáin*, a play in Irish by Pádraic Pearse. Once a visiting Brother, dressed as a Chinaman, performed wonderful magic tricks. Another time the famous Shakespeare actor Val Vousden performed extracts from *Hamlet* and *The Merchant of Venice*, and recited epic poems such as Tennyson's *The Charge of the Light Brigade*. His deep resonant voice, perfect diction, dramatic gestures and facial expressions were most impressive. Watching him, I renewed my resolve to become an actor when I grew up. Not surprisingly, 'actor' was top of my mental list of prospective careers.

Because the ground sloped away from the school building, our football pitch had a sharp decline. The Brothers tried to level the pitch by transferring topsoil in buckets from the higher to the lower end, utilising the whole school as a workforce. The work took many weeks, with hardly any improvement to show for it. It was months before the grass grew and the ground was playable again. We had eight football teams: Whites, Blacks, Reds and Blues, each of which had senior and junior teams. I was in the Blues, and I have to admit to being more of a hindrance than an asset. The truth is, I hated playing football. It wasn't my fault. I couldn't get football boots to fit me. I was the only boy to take size ten, and nine was the largest size available. How I managed to squeeze my feet into football boots is a mystery, but I can tell you that having to kick a hard leather ball with my feet squashed as in a vice, my big toes throbbing like a couple of boils, was far from pleasant. On wet days it was worse, when the ball was sodden and weighed half a ton. Small wonder that my aim was to avoid the ball at all costs. I became the butt of everyone's jokes when I was heard to say in panic as a boy was about to pass the ball, 'Don't give it to me, I don't want it.'

The captain of the Blues was a brilliant player nicknamed 'Spuggy' Power. I don't know his proper name. Off the field he was slow and soft-spoken, friendly and quiet. He gave me great encouragement, and almost convinced me that I wasn't as bad a player as I imagined. On the field, however, it was another story: he was nimble, alert, and showed an aggressiveness towards the opposing side that was altogether out of character. On the field too he was different towards me entirely, and never once attempted to curb his impatience and annoyance. I stretched his friendship to the limits. Our association in sport had to end; he just had to face it. I could see it was a strain on the poor fellow to break the news to me.

'I've something to tell ye . . . I'm real sorry, Joe, but ye see . . . that is . . . well, I hope you understand . . . '

'What is it?' I said, as if I didn't know.

'I'm afraid I have to drop ye off the team.'

I was greatly relieved to hear it, but didn't want it to show. 'Ye mean I'm dropped for good?'

''Fraid so. It can't be helped. I have . . . erm . . . to give another fella a chance.'

Poor Spuggy. He was so embarrassed. And I didn't have the wit to make it easy for him by being honest. He had needed Brother George's permission to drop me, and it came to my ears that, to justify his request, he had told him, 'It isn't fair. None of the other teams has a player that bad.' Brother George offered no objections; in fact he agreed a bit too readily, I thought. (He'd have known how badly I played, of course, for he refereed every match.) All told, I think I hid my relief very well.

In refereeing the games, Brother George was anything but

impartial, but nobody minded in the least. Once a goal or point was scored, he came in on the side of the underdogs, urging and encouraging them to level up. 'Come on there Tar Ball, that's it. Over to Philip, he's waiting for it. Great shot. Now Phil, up along the side. Good lad.' I admired that man to such an extent that I tried to emulate him without realising I was doing so, so that ever since then I have tended to sympathise with the weak, and to lean on the side of the loser – and not only in sport!

A new Brother came to the school and brought some welcome innovations. Brother Keegan was his name. Like Brother Arthur, he was a schoolboy at heart. We were frightened at first because of his bulky, swarthy appearance and blustery manner, but we soon came to revere him as much as we did the other Brothers. He introduced athletics to the school, and had everyone in training: running, high-jumping and 'hop-step-and-leppin'.' After weeks of this, he announced that we were going to have a 'Sports Week', and promised great prizes for the winners. We embraced the idea with gusto, for nothing like it had been seen in the school before.

The beauty of it was that we could enter whatever events we chose, and to cap it all we could even compete in bare feet, because all events would be held on grass. Thus encouraged, I entered my name for practically everything. Alas! If only my skill had been equal to my enthusiasm.

Brother Keegan was a remarkable man, although probably the world's worst organiser. He took charge of the whole affair on his own, not seeking assistance from anyone. All events were badly planned and a lot of time was lost. Not surprisingly, things became chaotic. By bluster and authoritative airs he managed to give the impression of being in full control, whereas in reality it was 'hit and miss and see what happens'. To make up for lost time he wouldn't allow anything, even heavy rain, to interfere with events. Despite this, 'Sports Week' lasted a fortnight. Nor did he think of having the field measured and marked out by white lines – or if he did, he didn't bother doing it. As a result, we had no idea of the length of a race, which must have been entered on his pile of papers simply as 'long' or 'short'. He would blow his whistle and demand silence, and when it came – eventually – he'd declare the next event, call those involved to gather around him, and announce, 'Now lads, line up and give me your names. Next race is two laps of the field' or 'From here to where those two amadhauns have the tape. *Will ye hold the blessed tape up off the ground!* Run down and tell them someone . . . If I lay me hands on them – God grant me patience!'

The tape should have been held taut and breast-high by two small boys stationed a hundred yards or so down the field, but growing tired of the endless wait, they moved close to-gether for a chat. With a short blast of the whistle the race was off. At once the Brother moved to his movie camera on a tripod and began to turn the handle, invariably missing the start. Oliver Hammet ran like a hare down the sloping field, face upturned to the sky, blinded by enthusiasm. What he was thinking of I'll never know, for even when he had breasted the tape he conti-nued to run, until he was smack in the middle of a stagnant pond, from which he emerged covered from head to toe in foul-smel-ling green slime and frog spawn. Happening to be close by the Brother, I was detailed to give Oliver a hand in cleaning him-self, though seeing the state he was in, God alone knew how I was going to manage it. By good fortune we met Brother White – the Brother with the impenetrable English accent – on his way to the farm. Taking matters in hand, he sent me to the store-room for a change of clothes, which he said I was to bring down to the 'kew beer'.

'The "kew beer"?' I asked myself. 'Where the hell's that? Does he mean the cow byre?'

'The cow byre, did you say sir?'

'Yes, are you doife?' In the cow byre Oliver had stripped off all his clothes, and the Brother was hosing him down with strong jets of water from a rubber hose. The cow byres were swilled down every day with the hose. I hadn't seen a nude boy since Kilkenny, and I can't describe my feelings as I barged in with the bundle of clothes and unavoidably noticed the hair on Oliver's body. Not realising that it was a natural development, I had been plagued for months with anguish over similar hair on my own body. I dreaded the jeering I'd get should my new blemish be discovered. As Oliver struggled his wet body into dry clothes, I waited outside. What a relief to realise that this had to do with growing up, and that it was one of those things that came with 'getting a man's voice'. My months of secret anxiety were dispelled, and it consoled me to know that every boy my age was suffering the same mental turmoil.

Back at the sports we were in time to see a race in which a tall lad named Butterly was running ahead of the field like an ostrich pursued by a fleet of lions. No one could catch him. (Appropriately, he hailed from Rush, County Dublin.) His speed in the longer events was amazing – well in front by long, easy strides, he was a sight to see, even from behind. Luckily the others had an advantage in the shorter races, which finished before he could get going, or he'd have scooped the lot. To this day, whenever I see the three-legged logo of the Isle of Man I'm reminded of Butterly.

I never enjoyed anything as much as those chaotic days of the sports – the many events I took part in: 'long' and 'short' races, high jump, 'hop-step-and-lep', wheelbarrow race, sack race, three-legged race, egg-and-spoon race (potato-and-spoon, actually) and relay races. Brother Keegan introduced rounders for the first time and included it in the programme of events. Even as the teams competed, he was explaining the rules.

If one thought the sports week was chaotic, then the prize-giving ceremonies were an utter shambles, although there was some attempt at observing a bit of formality and class. For instance, we wore our Sunday best, although it was a weekday, and the community of Brothers were invited. Where the prizes came from, heaven only knows. Apart from balls, mouth organs and hurley sticks (although the game wasn't played in the school), there were useless items like glass ashtrays and salt-

and-pepper sets. An assortment of cups and medals held pride of place on the display table, but close examination revealed inscriptions for activities far removed from our sports events. For instance, a boy got a cup that had once been awarded for a yachting event, and others got medals for singing or dancing.

Prize-giving was the most disorganised event ever witnessed. There were hold-ups galore while sheaves of paper were being leafed through. All offers of help were declined. My prize was a fountain pen. This is the only prize I ever won in my life, before, during or since sports week, so it may be supposed that I should have no trouble remembering why I won it, but I don't. Nor did I know at the time. I can only surmise that it might have been for some team event rather than an individual one, or I'd surely remember. (Pride won't admit of the possibility that I got it by mistake.)

The presentation of prizes was filmed, needless to say, and the film was shown in the recreation hall, projected onto a bedsheet hung from the ceiling. It caused riots of fun because of the comical way we all bobbed up and down like ducks on a choppy pond. This, despite the Brother's shouted commands – while filming – to 'walk slower – *slower* – SLOWER, I said. God grant me patience!' If we'd slowed any more we'd have been walking backwards.

Silent-film shows were a regular feature after this, for which Brother Keegan hired films starring Rin Tin Tin the clever German shepherd dog, or an equally clever chimpanzee. The chimp's antics had us standing on the chairs as he untied the heroine who had been bound to the railway tracks by a moustachioed villain in top hat and cloak. Meanwhile, a steam train was careering down the line towards them, while all we could do was shout, 'Hurry up, for God's sake!' Needless to say, the chimp succeeded just in time. That chaos reigned in the film shows too goes without saying, what with the constant breakdowns. This Brother was the proud owner of a film showing the Berlin Olympic Games of 1936, the year before, and we never tired of seeing it. We cheered for Jesse Owens, the American star runner, although some boys claimed that our own Butterly (or Butter-fly, as we now called him) would give Jesse a ton.

Our sporting heroes of those days were Jim Braddock, and Max and Buddy Baer, the heavyweight boxers; Danno Mahony, the world-famous wrestler, born in Kerry; and Lory Meagher, the Kilkenny hurler who was a legend even then, and who was spoken of and written about with a reverence that might have been envied by some of the saints in heaven. It was impossible to avoid having an interest in sport; it was a constant topic of conversation, and many boys had newspaper cuttings of their heroes or favourite teams pasted in old copybooks. Gaelic was the only football played in the school, although most of us had a favourite soccer team, based on which area of the city it came from. Mine was James' Gate, because my mother lived in James' Street then.

15

SUNDAY WALKS AND THE ANNUAL RETREAT

On Sundays we dressed in our good suits, clean shirts and long stockings, giving special care to the shirt-collar as we slid a celluloid stiffener into a groove behind each of the 'peaks' to prevent curling. However brightly one's boots shone, or one's hair gleamed in hair oil, the whole effect was lost if one's collar-points curled up. The difference between a neat and an untidy appearance depended on the state of the collar. Sometimes we pressed it between the pages of a book and slept on it for a night or two, but secretly, because the practice was forbidden.

In summer we didn't have this bother because we wore short-sleeved shirts with collar attached, and over this a woollen jumper. The uniform of black jersey and Eton collar had been discarded when Brother George became Superior. Our winter Sunday gear had the addition of jacket and overcoat.

Polishing our boots was an essential preparation for the Sunday walk. It was a major chore, especially if we had been weeding on the farm or gathering potatoes the previous week. We were issued with bootblacking in small paper-wrapped bars, like halfpenny bars of toffee, and they might as well have been toffee for all the good they were as boot polish. It had to be moistened first, then rubbed on the boots, which then had to be brushed vigorously for ages – literally 'spit and polish'. No wonder several lads preferred to spend their money on Cherry Blossom shoe polish instead of sweets. That got a great shine up, and with minimal brushwork.

It was now almost eleven o'clock. We formed into double file, each picking his companion for the walk, and away we started down the avenue to the public road, one long serpentine shape of boys winding along on our fifteen-mile walk. We wouldn't be back until three, in time for dinner. At every road junction the leaders looked back to the Brother for an indication of which way to turn. We walked on the footpath, where there was one, and Brother George stayed to the rear, on the road. Motor traffic in those days was light, and posed no threat to his safety. When it rained, we halted to his whistle to shelter under hedgerows and trees until it passed. When it persisted, we continued, hardly noticing it, unless it became so heavy that we had to take the shortest route home.

Our walks varied every week. Sometimes we went out through the east gate and via Glenageary, Sallynoggin and Glasthule to Dalkey, into Victoria Park and up the hill to the Folly. There we enjoyed the panoramic view over the Vale of Shanganagh and Killiney Bay. Young though we were, the beauty of the scene was not lost on us, and we lingered for about ten minutes. 'They say it's more beautiful than Naples,' the Brother once said. As we had heard the phrase 'See Naples and die', we thought it was great praise for a spot we called our own.

Another route was by the north gate towards Dean's Grange Cross, up the hill to Foxrock Church – then under construction – and if we took a right turn there, we walked along Stillorgan Road for several miles, down Booterstown Avenue, and home via Blackrock, Dún Laoghaire and Mounttown. If we turned left at the church, we went through Cornellscourt and Cabinteely, around Shankill Church, and home by Ballybrack, passing Lourdes TB Hospital. Our school band had a special relationship with the hospital, and gave many recitals for the patients. We played to an empty quadrangle, our audience's applause eerily descending from wards and open verandas overhead.

The long walks never bored or tired us, despite endless stretches of country road, with only hedges and fields on either side. Our walking pace was nice and steady, neither too brisk nor too slow, regulated by the Brother, who sent a runner from the rear up to the leaders when necessary.

Here and there could be glimpsed a beautiful manor house in landscaped garden, peeping from behind trees and high walls. They were relics of a grander age, their owners probably belonging to the 'old order' who opted to stay after the British handed back the country to the 'Free Staters'. Some new houses were beginning to sprout here and there, and I particularly recall new bungalows near Mounttown where advertising hoardings proclaimed their purchase price: £350. There were also four-bedroomed semi-detached houses costing £850. Boredom had no place on our walks, because we talked about films seen on the August or Christmas holidays. Until I had seen my first film, which was later than many of my companions, I recounted stories from the school library books. I loved reading, whereas my companions thought it belonged in the classroom.

By way of a change, we played 'car spotting', a game based on the registration plates of the motor cars passing on the road. The most frequent car-registration letters of the period were Z, ZZ and ZA, and we declared our choice of letters before setting off. The registrations appearing most often decided the winner, whose prize was to take all the loser's meat at dinner. Many a meatless dinner had I, thanks to that perishing game. Motor cars were not so numerous, and sometimes there were long intervals between them, so a lot of the enjoyment of the game lay in the suspense, waiting for a car to come into view, with side bets on what 'reg' it would carry. I'm sure our cheers puzzled many a passing driver.

We envied the 'outsiders' we met: children with their parents, or riding 'fairy' bicycles, although my special object of envy was always a boy with a dog, for my heart was set on owning a dog some day. Indeed, for most of my adult life I have in fact owned a dog.

Brother George sometimes invited a boy to accompany him on the roadway, and I was delighted to be chosen many times. He spoke about our system of government, the various government departments and their responsibilities, state finances, the budget, labour exchanges and their functions, the dole and so on. My comments and questions often made him roar with laughter. Once, when the subject was about the law, courts, prisons and suchlike, I mentioned that I had read a curious item in the paper recently: a man up in court for burglary had asked for three other charges to be taken into account. That man was mad, I told him, for doing such a thing.

'If I were that fellow,' I said, 'I'd be telling the judge about the times I had resisted temptation, the times I could have robbed but didn't. I'd tell how good I was, not how bad. Picture me up before the Master for, say, talking in class. Can you see me saying, "Sir, as you have the stick in your hand, do you know the store window that got broken?"

'And he'd say, "Was that you?"

'"Afraid so, *and* the apples stolen from the orchard too."

'"You again?"

'"Yes, sir."

'Well, I'd get three whacks on one hand for talking, same again on the other for the window, and probably "bend over" for the apples – three punishments instead of one. If only I'd kept me mouth shut.' It puzzled me why the Brother laughed so much, until he explained the mystery.

In the village of Kill O' The Grange there is a picturesque church whose Church of Ireland congregation was usually arriving for Sunday service about the time we were setting off. A number of parishioners, obviously well-to-do, were at that hour grouped outside the church door. They always turned friendly, smiling faces towards us, and kept up their greeting until the long procession passed. The ladies, in bright coloured dresses and picture hats, gestured demurely with gloved hands; the dark-suited gentlemen raised bowler hats by the brim in salute. Gratefully we smiled and waved in return; the Brother, his face scarlet with embarrassment, acknowledged their salutes by raising his soft felt hat several times.

What is particularly memorable about that gesture of friendship is that it was made by such people towards the like of us, the lowest of the low. All of us had suffered rejection by society in our more tender years, and that gesture of friendship left lasting impressions on us. I met a former school companion in

O'Connell Street around 1970 and most of our chat about 'old times' was taken up largely by that incident. It was a highlight in our school days – something we looked forward to whenever our Sunday walk took us by the village church. Such a great compliment towards the likes of us – paid by such lofty people, strangers – meant a lot – more in fact than I can say even now. The friendly greeting of these Protestants was most unusual in its day; it anticipated the ecumenical era by about thirty years. Further, our own Brother Treacy (I'll introduce him later) and the vicar of that church were good friends, and went for evening walks together. To this day I regret not having written to the vicar after I left school to let him know how much we appreciated his kindness and that of his parishioners.

It amused us to see Brother George's red face as he lifted his hat passing the group, for he was very shy with strangers; how often did we smile at his embarrassment when he greeted boys' families on visiting day. Lee had a camera and would take your photo and have it developed for fourpence, but he never succeeded in taking Brother George's picture, though he often tried. It was a box camera, and photographing someone was a slow business in those days, the subject having to co-operate and 'pose' by keeping quite still.

On fine days in summer we headed for the west pier in Dún Laoghaire. Halfway along the harbour wall there is an opening through which we went down some stone steps to a rocky slope. Although exposed to the whole of Dublin Bay, it was very private, being a good distance from the nearest point of shoreline at Salthill and Seapoint. We were the only people to use the spot as a bathing place, so we had it to ourselves. On the rocks we stripped into knee-length black showering trunks, and at low tide anyone could get in the water, which came only to our waists. When it was 'full in', however, on alternate weeks, only those able to swim were allowed in, for it was deep at this point. The rest of us had to sit on the rocks and watch for an hour or so. A new boy, to whom nobody apparently had explained this, once got into difficulties in the water and almost drowned, surrounded though he was by many swimmers, and with an audience of a few hundred sitting on the rocks. It was Brother George who spotted the boy in trouble and jumped in, fully clothed, to rescue him.

Sometimes for a change we swam at Salthill and Seapoint, where non-swimmers could get in even at full tide, and we shared those spots with the public. What I didn't like about swimming were the contortions we had to go through in observing strict standards of modesty when dressing. It was worse at the west pier, when we had to keep our balance on the rocky slope in windy conditions. After the swim we bought 'lovely oranges, two-a-penny' from women in black shawls beside the railway level crossing. As usual, those who bought them shared them around, so we all benefited.

Every year the school went on retreat. We didn't actually go any-where: a visiting priest from a preaching order – the Franciscans, Dominicans, or Oblates – came in place of the chaplain and gave a series of sermons. 'Missioners', they were called. After the rosary and usual prayers in the evening, the visiting priest began to preach, going on for about an hour. The trick was to stay awake. I couldn't concentrate for that length in church, and soon nodded off. If I were awake itself, my mind was elsewhere, revelling in the adventure story of my current library book. Besides, the subject of the sermons didn't attract us in the least – far from it – so we couldn't switch off too soon.

Every year we heard the same old thing: death, hell, pain and punishment. It was amazing how the missioners chose this topic every year, and no matter how they dressed it in flowery language and dramatic gestures, there was no disguising it. And didn't they love the drama – pacing up and down, waving their arms about. Their voices thundered in the rafters one minute and dropped to a whisper the next. We looked up, thinking they were finished. Some hope! All their fancy phrases and footwork were wasted. We tired of hearing the same old thing year after year, so we either switched off or nodded off. Of course, I was all right at the back of the chapel, where I had to be, to play the harmonium for the hymn and Benediction when the sermon was over. It was the poor unfortunate gobdaws up at the front that I pitied, trapped right under the missioner's nose, unable to fidget or take a nap. It must have been hell for them and no mistake.

One year, however – my last winter in school – saw a retreat that was exceptional in every way. For a start, there were none of the usual dramatics, ranting and raving – the opposite in fact, for we had to concentrate to hear the soft, gentle voice of this missioner. His name was Father Allen, one of the Oblates from Inchicore. We warmed to him straightaway, and as he was smaller in stature than some of the senior boys, there was an instant rapport between him and us. It was notable too in that he never mentioned hellfire – not once! The usual themes of death, dying and eternal damnation had no place in his sermons throughout the week. Furthermore, he wasn't one for parading up and down inside the altar rails, but was perched, content, on a high stool for the evening. Nor did he preach, really, but spoke in ordinary, natural tones, quietly and in simple language – not about a fierce God, a punishing God, a vengeful God – but about a gentle, kind God full of compassion and love, a God whose mercy knew no bounds. He told us too of the extraordinary power of prayer, and the special place of Mary and her influence with God. He embellished his talks with anecdotes to hold our interest. We could indeed have listened all night without stress or strain, and when he finished we felt like applauding – which was unheard of in those days.

Such was its dynamism, its impact, that it doesn't surprise me that I remember the retreat after nearly seventy years. And yet, there was an unpleasant aftermath which I have to mention: any boy who fell foul of the Master for weeks afterwards got double punishment 'for forgetting the little man from Inchicore, and lapsing into your old ways so soon.'

For the Master was present, hidden in the dim light under the gallery overhang. He was out of place, I thought, because of his cruelty. He was a bully: devious, wily and fly, scheming, artful and sly. He used his rod with sadistic relish, coolly and without losing his temper – rather, with a smile or smirk. I saw him as a gatecrasher, an intruder in the special preview of heaven intended exclusively for us boys. I know that pain and fear were the lot of children in all schools at the time, but many teachers went too far, and the Master was one of them.

16

KITES

Brother George posted a notice promising a shilling to any boy who could make a successful kite unaided. By 'successful', he meant one that would stay up in the air a long time. Most boys had never seen a kite before, so the offer got hardly any response, which was just as well because there wasn't much of a scramble for the materials. I had never seen a kite before either, but I did know what a kite looked like, from a picture I had once seen in a book.

I asked Father Burke if he could get me some brown paper, I 'found' a few pieces of light sticks in the carpenters' shop, 'borrowed' a bottle of stuff called 'gum Arabic' from the library, bought a ball of string for tuppence in Woolworths, and thus managed to get the materials together. After a day or two most of the other lads gave up for one reason or another – the paper was wrong, or the sticks, they couldn't get any twine, or 'Who needs a silly old kite anyway?' – leaving me to contend for the prize with only one boy. But he happened to be Willie Morrison.

Willie was brilliant. He knew everything – indeed, he did not really need to go to school. He was only ever wrong once in his life, and that was when he gave me a wrong prompt. We were reading in school about this Greek fellow who made some important discovery in his bathwater and shouted 'Eureka!' The Master asked me what that meant and, prompted by Willie, I replied, 'Where's the soap?'

Men like Willie are so rare, it seems there can be only one or two of them in the world at a time, every half century or so. Here are a couple of examples from the past. A dapper young man in the clubhouse at St Andrew's was being congratulated by everyone on having achieved the impossible: a hole-in-one on the par seven (you know the one – with the double dog-leg, six sand bunkers and a lake). He was called to the telephone. 'Oh, thank heaven I've reached you,' the caller said, all out of breath. 'It's St Mackintosh's Hospital here. We've an acute case of eucharabibitis – ten-year-old son of a Maharajah – only you can save him – last known case occurred – '

'Yes, I know – 1875. See you in a jiffy.'

No need to guess the rest; it's now medical history. Ten-hour operation, boy literally at death's door when our hero pulls him through, 'our hero' being Willie Morrison, though in this case he was known as Sir William Morrison, Bart, KG, FRCS (and a string of other letters a yard long).

A century earlier, an innocent man languished in jail in America charged with a particularly vicious murder, so vile a crime that the crowd tried to break in to lynch him. The evidence was so bad that it seemed nothing or no one could save him. But wait! We're forgetting! There was one man, one alone in the wide world who could do just that; one who, unknown to the wretched accused, had been conducting his own investigations behind the scenes. 'Something about the case didn't smell right,' he said afterwards. Yes, this internationally renowned amateur criminologist, master of his craft, this criminal lawyer, genius of jurisprudence, never known to fail, *he* was the man who was to grasp the reins of the defence firmly in his hands. Imagine, if you can, the immense relief which engulfed the young accused, his beautiful wife and six children on hearing the news.

America came to a standstill for the trial. All eyes scanned the newspapers, in which was described every nuance, every inflection in the master's words, every gesture of his manicured hands. So tense was the courtroom drama that that vast nation held its collective breath while the defence went about dismantling – demolishing stone by stone, brick by brick – the carefully constructed edifice of damning evidence until, in a spectacular climax, he proved conclusively that the real murderer had a severe squint, spoke Sanskrit with a lisp, and dragged his left leg, a description which came nowhere near to fitting his client. And where was that evidence skilfully uncovered, you want to know? In the real culprit's fingerprints, that's where! In the words of the defence, it was 'as plain as the nose on the judge's face' (and that worthy wasn't known as 'the Beak' for nothing).

The 'not guilty' verdict was pronounced to thunderous applause, led by the judge himself. America went back to business and resumed normal living, but not before it had breathed one enormous sigh of relief, the like of which had never been known in living memory. So gigantic a sigh was it that, not surprisingly, it was felt on the other side of the Atlantic in Ireland, and has come down in that country's history as '*Oíche na Gaoithe Mhóire*' ('the Night of the Big Wind').

And the advocate's name? Willie Morrison, of course, known far and wide as 'Big Bill' – after the size of his fee, some said. And seeing that he was only five foot five in his socks, they may have had a point.

Mark my words, a Willie Morrison comes only once or twice in a lifetime. You should look out for him, because another one of his breed is due to make an appearance any day. You'll be able to spot him easily by the brilliant way he accomplishes whatever he turns his hand to.

Well, didn't we have a WM in our school. Needless to say, he shone in all school subjects, although like me he hated maths. He said it was a sheer waste of good playtime to be stuck in the classroom twisting his brain in knots figuring out problems like: 'If a brick weighs ten pounds and half a brick, how much would five bricks weigh?' when all you had to do was weigh the silly things. And I must say, I agreed with him. If you thought him clever in class though, it was nothing compared to his knowledge of important things – things like soccer players, cricketers, racing drivers, horses and jockeys, birds, animals, fishes, insects, flowers, plants, trees, national flags and, of course, battleships. I'll tell you about them in a minute. On these subjects he was an unrivalled authority, everybody's private consultant.

And how, you ask, did Willie come by this boundless store of knowledge? Well, I'll tell you. By studying the 'blank' sides of Player's cigarette cards, that's how! They were small cards found in every packet of John Player's cigarettes (one in a pack of ten, two in a twenty). One side showed a coloured picture of the subject, and on the other you read all about it in tiny print. The cards came to the school via visiting relatives, and while the rest of us – the goms, the eejits – used the cards as play-things in various games, as I told you already, Willie collected them and put them to better use by harvesting their crop of knowledge. Willie was like that.

He played the baritone in the school band. That, as you know, is a shrunken version of the euphonium, which in turn, is a shrunken version of the bass or tuba. If we weren't close chums itself, we were friends.

There was one subject about which Willie was crazy, and that subject was battleships. He had what you might call a hang-up about it, and if he had a fault at all it was that he was inclined to waffle on a bit too much if you let him. So much was he obsessed that he told me privately that he intended joining the British navy 'the very minute' he left school. Which he did. Mind you, he would have had to lie about his age to get in, but Willie wouldn't worry about a little thing like that.

Around this time (1936 or early 1937), a German battle-ship, the *Schleswig Holstein*, paid a courtesy visit to Ireland. She was a huge vessel – to us boys she was a monster – and pre-sumably because there wasn't enough depth of water to allow her to berth in Dún Laoghaire harbour or at the North Wall in Dublin she dropped anchor a few miles offshore in Scotsman's Bay between Dún Laoghaire and Sandycove. On 'children's visit-ing day' the entire school were taken to the battleship on the *Royal Iris*, a pleasure boat which in those days was a familiar sight, cruising around Dublin Bay, always with coloured bunt-ing flying gaily from her rigging.

Two of the German naval officers spoke English of a sort. I suppose a few others might have done so as well, but we in

Willie's little group collared the two of them that definitely did, and I remember their surprise and embarrassment when Willie began barraging them with technical questions. How he thought them up I do not know. Nor was he content asking them about their own ship; he pestered them about every vessel in their navy – type and number and so on, you know the sort of thing. I suppose you could say that he had an inquisitive mind. Purely innocent, I promise. I mean, he wasn't spying or anything; he just wanted to compare the German and British fleets and learn more about his favourite subject. So he said afterwards. I was leaning against the halyard, or the bulkhead, or the barnacle, or whatever you call the wall in a battleship, watching Willie battling it out with the Germans, a buffer between us and them like a knight of King Arthur's court (I forget which one – I haven't read the book in a while). Mind you, I wasn't half puzzled listening to him going on about the ship's eleven-inch guns when, from where I was standing, they seemed to be a lot longer than that. But I didn't correct him, not wishing to interrupt, seeing that he was holding the floor – or the deck, I should say. I mentioned it on the way home, but all I got for my trouble was a look up to the sky, and 'Oh boy!' Or it could have been 'Oh buoy!' Whichever it was, I wasn't any the wiser. I needn't tell you the Germans weren't pleased about their bombardment and showed it too, leaving a small group of schoolboys gaping at their retreating backs. That Willie's knowledge grew no greater that day was no fault of his.

This courtesy call by a German battleship came only a few years before the Second World War, when a series of Player's cigarette cards then current in the school featured warships of the British navy. (Though to be fair, I don't think Player's knew that the war was coming. *We* certainly didn't.) The cards showed a battleship, man-of-war, cruiser, dreadnought, frigate or destroyer, and the reverse or 'blank' side gave, in tiny print, full information about the vessel: how many of its class were in the Royal Navy, tonnage, maximum speed, and the number, emplacement and size of its guns. In fact, all the data which, if it were current, an enemy or potential enemy would give his right arm to have. The likely explanation is, I imagine, that the warships were old, obsolete vessels, so no harm was done. Anyway, we boys in Willie Morrison's little group were extremely put out by the Germans' refusal to give any information, especially as the British were so generous with theirs.

To get back to the kites, for it seems I can't put off telling you about them any longer. (You'll understand my reluctance when I say that it was one of the most embarrassing days of my whole life.) My kite was finished, so I went along to see how Willie was getting on with his. I was goggle-eyed. 'What in the name of all that's holy is that?' I jeered. 'It looks like a box with no ends.'

'That's what it is, a box kite. Haven't you ever heard of a box kite?' he answered with a superior tone. Willie was like that.

'There's no such thing. I happen to know that kites look like this,' I said, showing him my diamond-shaped one. 'I saw one in a book once, and anyway, you're not seriously expecting that oul' yoke to fly, are you?' I had to laugh at the good of it. 'I mean to say, where's its wings? And it hasn't even a tail!'

'We'll see right now if it'll fly or not,' he said, not a bit upset by my sneering, 'for it's finished as well.' Off went the pair of us to the football fields, attracting the father and mother of crowds on the way. The whole school gathered round us in next to no time, including Brother George. Willie's kite captured all the attention and drew a fair amount of questions as well. Nobody had eyes for mine at all. Said I to myself, 'Poor Willie, he's going to get a terrible death when his box fails to fly. How can he of all people be so wrong?'

We posted ourselves at opposite ends of the field so as not to foul our lines, the horde of boys having to man the sidelines as if they were watching a football final. After a few false starts, both kites were soon sailing aloft, to the tremendous excitement and cheers of the school. To my amazement, Willie's box kite soared and swooped and looped the loop, and gave a powerful display – and did so for many a day. Alas! My master-piece was short-lived, for didn't it come crashing down in smithereens, having fallen apart after hardly a minute. I got no sympathy – quite the reverse, for the jeering I had shortly before predicted as Willie's inevitable lot was now targeted on me. Only more so. Red-faced, I gathered up my bits and pieces and set off to greet the successful Morrison with 'more power', but as I was walking the mile-long (so it seemed) football pitch, didn't some perishing blighter start whistling 'Colonel Bogey' in time to my step, and soon the whole school joined in. I was mortified. Did you ever dream you were walking abroad in public with nothing on, only a short shirt which kept flapping up and down in the breeze to your horrible embarrassment? Mortified? I nearly died! What harm, only I needn't have bothered going along with my congratulations, because Willie didn't notice a bit of me when I reached him, that busy he was, threading his string through a small bit of paper which bore a command to 'BOMB THE SCHOOL'. In amazement, everyone watched the message slowly being hoisted up the line by the upward draughts of air, like a flag ceremoniously climbing a flagpole. When it reached the kite up in the clouds, there was a mighty cheer. Willie was like that, full of novel ideas, and he could make lots of other things too, like hats, and gliders, and sailing boats, all out of old newspapers.

Needless to say, he scooped the shilling prize that day. Crafty oul' fox! He used Scotch tape on his kite, whereas I stuck mine with liquid gum. Where I went wrong was in not waiting a day or two for the gum to dry. 'I could have told you that,' Willie said with smug authority, 'if you'd only asked.'

'It would have made no difference,' I said, 'for wouldn't you have got the prize just the same, because yours would have been first up while mine was drying.'

'Wrong again,' Willie said. 'You could have claimed a prize too, 'cos if you remember, the Brother promised a shilling to whoever made a kite that could fly. He said nothing about being first. Have a look at the notice again.' He was right, of course, and for being as clever as all that, I hated him for that minute.

17

CORNCRAKES AND PIGEONS

The boy who played the harmonium in the chapel left the school, and I was chosen to succeed him. Why the bandmaster picked me I'll never know, for he had no reason to believe that I had any love for the instrument – which I hadn't. Lee said the bandmaster decided by the shape of your teeth what instrument you played, but how that applied to the harmonium was a mystery to me. In any case, Willie Redmond couldn't have been more wrong in his selection, for I couldn't make a fist of it at all. He had me practising most of the time on a piano in the sixth classroom, probably because he couldn't very well shout at me in the chapel. You should have seen his face: it turned purple, and as for his neck, it bloated to twice its size from frustration, the sinews fit to burst his collar, and he'd wring his hands and puff and blow and snort, and yell 'how sorely' I was trying his patience. It was a pity we were on our own, for the other fellows would have paid to see his performance. He placed a penny on the back of each of my hands when I practised, and when one fell off you wouldn't believe how much pain that caused him.

Once, his temper getting the better of him, he struck the back of my hand sharply with the edge of a foot rule, but when the lesson ended he apologised politely. I was flabbergasted by this rare show of concern about me, for it gave me a peek into his personal nature which emboldened me to confide that my problem in playing the piano that day was that the Master had given me a fierce hiding an hour before, which had left the fingertips of both my hands tender and swollen. At the same time I begged him not to say anything about it, or make a complaint in my name. 'I'm afraid of what the Master will do to get his own back,' I explained.

'I think Brother George should be told,' he said. 'I'd tell him for you myself, except that I can't be seen to interfere.'

'I was sure you'd take the Master's side,' I said.

'No fear of that. That man called me a bastard a long time ago – when I was your age, in fact – and I've never forgotten.'

Nothing passed between us for ages. He was probably re-living the experience; I was wondering what he meant.

But sore fingers were not always the cause of my slow progress on the harmonium. The trouble was that I had two hands which liked to do things independently. My left could manage the bass clef on its own without a bother – well, after one or two stabs at the exercise. Likewise, after a few goes, my right hand on its own, unencumbered by the left, was well able to rattle off the melodies and arpeggios. It was when I tried playing with both hands that the trouble started. They downright refused to cooperate with each other, which was my misfortune, and as if it weren't hard enough, having to play separate tunes with each hand, I also had to use my feet to pump two bellows under the harmonium, which wouldn't go at all without air. Through concentrating on my hands, I often forgot to work my feet, causing the tunes to dry up in a death rattle like a bagpipe's drone. The gallons of sweat I contributed to becoming a harmonium player I could swim in, if I was able to swim. I did try hard to get the hang of it, but in spite of all Willie Redmond's dancing and shouting, it was no go. You could have either the bass-clef music or the treble – and welcome – but not both together.

Happily, my problem with the instrument was to solve itself quite simply. It happened this way: the choir comprised about sixteen boys of various ages, and it seemed inevitable that there should always be one or two 'corncrakes' whose voices were on the brink of breaking. They were always a shade under the note, especially in the high register, never quite getting there, and the upshot was that before the choir was half-way through the first verse of a hymn, it was dragged down by a semitone, and into a lower key.

The struggle for supremacy between harmonium and choir, battling it out in different keys, was unbelievably hard on the ear, and I don't suppose I helped matters much by contributing the odd dissonant chord and bum note for good measure. Our uncharitable friends had a field day. I knew I'd get the blame. 'Hey Joe, are ye playin' that yoke with yer elbows again?' And of course there were the inevitable quips about the cat with its tail caught in the mangle, and the cinder that was stuck under the door. It couldn't go on. In the end, Brother George appealed to Willie Redmond. 'Can't you do something about that awful caterwauling, for heaven's sake?' he pleaded. 'It's worse than a dozen banshees abroad on Hallowe'en Night.'

And so it happened that I was told in future to play only a few bars' introduction to each hymn and then 'Let the choir carry on on their own,' which made it look as though it were my fault. I didn't complain; it suited me fine, because the most I needed to learn of any hymn from now on was four introductory bars, and I could just about manage that.

Mr Hubert Rooney of the Royal Academy of Music came for an hour once a week to train the choir – not in the chapel, for some reason, but in the sixth classroom, where two ancient pianos reposed peacefully when I wasn't hammering out my exercises. He was the recognised expert in the whole country on Gregorian chant or 'plainsong', which was mostly what the choir sang, in Latin of course. It mattered not that nobody (except Mr Rooney, I suppose) understood a single word. He probably came to us straight off the golf course, because he was dressed in a bright tweed jacket and plus fours, bow tie and cap. He was my idea of what it meant to be a 'gentleman'. He lived in a big house in its own grounds near Victoria Park in Dalkey, which we sometimes passed on our Sunday walks.

As school organist (which was what I was called, because it was easier to say than 'school harmoniumist'), I had to be present at rehearsals – why, I never knew, because I took no part. I hated it. If you had to stand for a whole hour looking down at sixteen tonsils and listening to what I heard, you'd understand. The choir bellowed gustily at the top of its voice, everyone trying to shout down the other. There was no piano accompaniment, so the loss of pitch was not noticeable at all – at least not to my ears. Mr Rooney didn't fail to notice, of course: it nearly broke the poor man's heart. He'd rush to the piano and strike the original chord, which turned out to be several tones higher than the key the choir were now in, for it was amazing the dragging-down effect which even one corncrake can have on a whole choir. Unfortunately, he was powerless to do anything about it. Oh, he identified the corncrake all right by a process of elimination, and was always very apologetic and polite when asking him to leave, but it wasn't long before someone else reached the age when his voice broke, so there was no getting rid of corncrakes entirely. Yet Mr Rooney never raised his voice, never once complained or became impatient – unless you count the odd painful intake of breath and raising of the eyes to heaven. If any man deserved a medal for patience, it was Mr Hubert Rooney!

Father Sylvester Burke was the school chaplain. I think I mentioned him before. It was his first appointment after ordination, so he was young and green. His chubby cheeks and shock of jet-black hair made him appear in his early twenties, but I'm sure he was older than that. He was always in the same good mood, friendly and chatty, not that we saw all that much of him outside daily Mass and weekly Confession, for he took no other part in the routine of the place. I, being an altar boy, had more contact with him than most, and yet I saw him rarely enough. One felt his presence all right, in a vague sort of way, somewhere on the outskirts of things. He seemed always to be passing by in the distance, never stopping.

Once, as I was leaving the box after Confession, he called me back to ask if I would like to go shooting pigeons. Well, you know yourself, a request from the priest was like a royal command. We set off for the woods beyond the farm, he with a double-barrelled rifle bent over his arm, me carrying a light box. I only accompanied him, you understand; he would be doing the shooting. I wasn't comfortable with the idea at all, thinking it wasn't right for a priest to take a gun to shoot poor birds, just for the sake of it.

'Can you eat pigeons, Father?' I asked on the way. It was just to open conversation – something to say. I didn't really want to know, to be honest. But never in all my life was I so sorry for asking a simple question like that.

'Why certainly Joe, did you not know that?' he answered in amazement. 'Dear oh dear oh dear! Yes, of course you can eat pigeons – and very tasty they are too.' Then, while he prepared and loaded the gun he resumed: 'Never tasted pigeon! We'll have to do something about that, now won't we? Tell you what, Joe, I'll bag one for your tea; it'll be a lovely treat for you.'

He was a hopeless shot, I was glad to see. You couldn't imagine how bad. He missed so often and wasted so many bullets we were almost giving up, having scared all the birds away, forever it seemed. And this suited me fine, because as I said, I felt bad about being there. But then he'd remember his promise to bag a pigeon for my tea and say how we'd have another go as soon as the birds came back. I could have bitten my tongue for asking if you could eat pigeons. 'A promise is a promise,' he kept repeating, and he stuck it out and waited and waited, until finally one bird, braver or more stupid than the rest, ventured back and flew straight into one of the priest's bullets.

Back we turned for home, me in the rear with the pigeon, and just in case pigeons had spirits I whispered, 'I'm sorry, really I am. It wasn't my fault, honest.' Never having been that close to a pigeon before, I saw how beautiful it was, and this made me feel more guilty. The priest led me to the main house and into the Brothers' basement kitchen, where he told me to place the bird on Cook's scrubbed deal table in the centre. As we entered, Cook was sitting by a black-leaded range set into a large alcove, which, along with a narrow wooden press and stone sink or trough, took up most of one side of the kitchen.

She was the Brothers' cook, and as the kitchen was out of bounds, we didn't know her name. She was Cook to us with a capital 'C'. Short, stout, bossy, and with a strong country accent, she was mistress of that kitchen; it was her '*sanctum sanctorum*', as she put it. She loved fancy words.

'Would you mind cooking this for Joe here?' the priest innocently asked. At first I didn't think she minded; the doubt would come presently.

'With the greatest of animosity, Father,' replied Cook with a broad smile. Although I didn't know what she meant, I thought it sounded nice. It might have been the smile.

'Would you believe it?' the priest went on. 'Joe here is after telling me that he has never tasted pigeon before. Imagine that!'

'Musha, avick,' Cook put her face close to mine, nearly nose to nose, 'and where in the wide world has the poor craythur been that he hasn't tasted pigeon before? How did he manage to reach the ripe old age of what – thirteen is it? – and not know the taste o' pigeon! My, my! Why, I bet ye what ye like even Friday's Dinner himself has ate pigeon at some time or other.' (Friday's Dinner was a poor scrawny beggar who came to the kitchen's back door for a 'bit o' dinner' on Fridays, and ate it outside in the sunken 'area' in hail, rain or snow. When finished, he'd beam a toothless, greasy smile of thanks up to the row of boys' faces peering down over the playground wall, and they'd throw the odd coppers down to him – itself a silent acknowledgement that, although they were poor themselves, here was a man who was worse off.)

Father Burke, annoyed or hurt by Cook's remarks, said, 'Now, Cook, there's no need to be like that at all, life's too short for that sort o' thing,' and to signal an end of the matter he added, 'Joe will be outside when it's ready; you can give him a shout. Come along, Joe.'

I was suspicious by now about Cook, and away I went to look up the word 'animosity' in the library dictionary, but as I couldn't spell it I couldn't find it, so I asked Brother Arthur.

He wanted to know where I had come across the word,

and when I told him, he said, 'Boys oh boys! Then I'd hate to be in your shoes, Joe. Cook's obviously mad at you. Sure that woman even eats Christian Brothers for her breakfast. Why on earth didn't you warn Father Burke about her?'

'But I never knew – '

'Take my advice and steer clear of that lady,' he said with a half-smile that left me wondering if he was pulling my leg. 'In fact, I wouldn't go back to her again if I were you.'

I was trembling when she sent for me to collect the cooked pigeon, and wouldn't have gone at all but for the goading of my friends, who of course were only thinking of themselves. It's a wonder I didn't choke on the bird. Not that there was much to choke on anyway. What I mean is, pluck the feathers off a pigeon and what have you got? Not much, I can tell you, especially when there's no shortage of fellows wanting a piece of it. From among those who devoured it I asked for a volunteer to bring back the plate, but they all ran off, leaving me to face the music alone. Timorously I thanked Cook very much, said it was the nicest thing I'd ever tasted, and turned to go.

'Wait a minit,' she snapped. 'Ye don't think yer gettin' off that light, do ye? There's a bucket o' wather an' a scrubbin' brush all ready for ye. Ye can get down on yer hands an' knees now, so ye can, an' return the favour be scrubbin' me flure.'

Down I got to wash the red tiles with a scrubbing brush and carbolic soap, and after half an hour, when I'd just about managed to clean a patch under a side table, about a yard square, Cook came quietly back, and with a shout that made me crack my head against the underside of the table she bawled, 'Glory bit o' God! An' will ye look at the tiny bit he's done afther all this time, I ask yer holy pard'n. Musha, an' is that the best ye can do?' Positioning herself with her back to the range, arms folded, she glowered down, waiting for some response, I suppose. I began scrubbing at a furious rate to make up for lost time. Seeing that she wasn't getting any excuses from me, she went on, 'All I can say is dis: I hope from de bottom o' me heart ye won't be dependin' for your livin' on scrubbin' flures when ye

148

*The author (right) in Carriglea,
with his friend 'Ape' (c. 1937)*

lave this place, for ye'll surely starve to deat', so ye will.' She paused to let that sink in. 'Look at here, I'm sure afther all dis time Brother George must be wondherin' if it's lost ye are entirely, so away with ye outa me sight this minit, before I land meself in the soup for keepin' ye here. An' if he asks yeh what yev been doin', for the luv o' Pete don't tell him yev been washin' *my* flure, for dat'd be a grave prevarication.'

As I climbed the steps from the 'area' to the playground, I could hear her voice. 'It bates Banagher, so it does, how some people t'ink they can waltz in here an' plonk dead pigeons down on *my* clean table, without as much as a . . . '

The story of the pigeon had by this time spread around the whole place, and as luck would have it, didn't I bump into Brother George, surrounded by a few cronies, as usual. He confronted me, his fingers threaded through each other across his chest, thumbs slowly rotating round one another (a posture he took when he was being sarcastic), and sniped good-naturedly: 'Well Joe, I hear you've been dining off pigeons, no less.'

'Pigeon, sir.' (I took things literally in my young days.)

'Hmm. Pigeon, then. And tell me, was it to your liking? How did you find it, pray?'

'I didn't find it, sir; Father Burke shot it.'

Shaking his head slowly, he walked away, muttering more to himself than to his little group: 'It's my own fault; I shouldn't have asked.'

I steered clear of Father Burke after that, and didn't go to Confession for a month in case I got another shooting invitation. Tar Ball and I were talking about Father Burke one day. He said he hated him, which I thought extreme. 'He gives out terrible hard penances at Confession, that's why,' he said. 'Is it the same with you?'

'Of course, but I don't mind that.'

'Well, maybe you deserve them, but I don't have any sins arawl to tell him. I suppose even if ye were one o' the angels theirselves outa heaven – Kerry Bim, and Sarah Flynn – ye'd get gev ten Our Fathers, ten Hail Marys, an' ten Glory Bits o' the Father. He'd have ya on yer knees prayin' all day, so he would, if he had his way. I'd hate to see what ye'd get for murder.'

I never found out Tar Ball's name. He was so called because of his scruffy appearance. He had spiky hair which stood on end like a porcupine's, even if he drenched it in hair oil. Because of their rough, cracked skin, his hands never looked clean, however hard he scrubbed them. The Brother once said he was 'like a ball of tar', and the name stuck.

150

It was easy to be lumbered with a nickname. One lad was called 'Biscuit' simply because he mispronounced the word as 'biscute' when reading aloud in an English lesson. Certain nicknames were tagged on because of a physical defect – unless of course it was a serious defect, in which case it was *never* referred to. For instance, Fahy had a stammer so bad that the poor chap's head nearly shook off his body when he was trying to get a word out. It was very sad to see, and no one would even think of jeering him. But a lesser defect or blemish – that was different entirely. For instance, Stiffer O'Brien – who played bass or tuba in the band – had a stiff left arm which stuck out from his side, and even when O'Brien was in the playground it remained that way, as if he thought he was still holding his instrument. Then there were two Mullhall brothers who suffered from flat feet. The older was 'Big Duck', and the younger, 'Little Duck'. It was easy to see by their huge size why a boy answered to 'Ape' and another to 'Zulu', but I could never figure out how 'Spuggy' got his name, or 'Paddy Whack', 'Funny Dumpling', or 'Tripound Cullen'. They didn't mind their nicknames, and answered to them when called, even by the Brothers.

18

CONFIRMATION

Our Confirmation was looming, and for months in advance we went 'all out' preparing for it – that is to say, all school subjects and trades were shelved for the time being. There was a large number of boys to be confirmed – probably half the school – and we were divided into several classes. I was in the Master's class, so I knew we were in for a rough time. Briefly, preparation for Confirmation entailed having to memorise the Catechism from cover to cover, word for word. The Catechism was a booklet comprised mostly of hundreds of questions and answers covering all aspects of 'the faith'; we had to study it to the point of being word-perfect.

With fingers in our ears we memorised every line, and when each page was mastered we had to undergo an oral test and suffer the inevitable sore fingers for the slightest lapse of memory or slip-up, or any departure from the precise wording. Over us hung the threat of exclusion from the sacrament of Confirmation if we failed the archbishop's catechism question on the day, with (of course) the direst of consequences. We had been given to understand that the bishop would simply pass over the unfortunate boy, who would then suffer a wait of three years until the next Confirmation ceremony in the area. Nor did it help us to know that we were going to be confirmed in Monkstown parish church, in full view of the public.

Clean and uncomfortable in new suits, kneeling in the church, we waited for the Archbishop of Dublin. By 'we' I mean close on three hundred boys, about half of whom were to be confirmed. Tension mounted. Fear of flunking our catechism test mounted too. It seemed years since we had come in.

Every occupied row had a long vacant seat in front. 'Five boys per seat,' we'd been told, 'and leave every other row vacant to allow the bishop to pass through to confirm each boy individually.'

We waited – and waited. Not a sound from three hundred boys in all that time! Amazing! But the patience of boys has its limits, and someone was tempting providence to breaking point. Inevitably came signs of restlessness – faint at first, suggested, imagined rather than real. The signs were bound to be noticed by Brother George, as indeed they were, almost at once, his senses honed to razor-sharpness by years of experience. To the inexpert eye, these signs meant nothing – just a few sporadic, timorous coughs and clearing of throats, the odd shuffle of feet. But to the ever-alert Brother George they were portents of disaster, tiny pebbles cascading from the mountaintop, harbingers of a dangerous landslide. His reaction was swift, amazingly simple and immediately effective – he whispered '*Sit down!*' and calamity was averted for the time being. The only ones to hear the order were the boys in the front row, so they were first to obey. The second row followed, then row after row after row, right back to us in the rear. Visually it resembled the ripple effect of a light breeze skimming over a field of corn, but the sound was indeed like that of a landslide. When the echoes died, we settled down to wait again.

After an age, something stirred behind us. Taking a chance, for we'd been warned on peril of our lives not to move a muscle, I looked around, impatient to get my first ever sighting of an archbishop. I'll never forget it! 'Why, he's ancient,' I whispered. 'He's a hundred years old if he's a day – easily the oldest man in the world. Look, fellas.' The bishop, surrounded by a dozen altar boys, might not have been visible at all but for his tall mitre, angled above the boys' heads at forty-five degrees. 'A minute or two more now,' I was thinking, 'and they'll be here.'

I was in the back row, nearest the door and therefore furthest from the altar, and I shared the seat with Spuggy, Ape and the Wynne twins. I looked up front again and, by stretching my neck, could see Brother George standing in the left side-aisle, his back to the wall, opposite the first row. He'd be moving towards us during the confirmations, I thought, in line with the archbishop so as to spot any boy who might flunk his catechism question. 'And woe betide that boy, whoever he may be,' he would say.

'What the hell are they doin' out there?' Spuggy wanted to know, prodding me impatiently.

'Can't ye hold yer hour?' I snapped. 'I heard ye. They're tryin' to sort theirselves out, I suppose – how am I to know?' Right enough, they seemed to be having a bit of trouble getting into position, for they were shuffling about. The archbishop, in flowing white and gold vestments, was bent nearly double with age, which accounted for the strange angle of his mitre. In his hand a long staff, crooked on top, helped him stay on his feet. The altar boys wore white surplices and black soutanes like Father Burke's.

At last they formed themselves in twos, the archbishop and chaplain taking up the rear. The organ played a burst of introduction, we all stood up to sing 'Come Holy Spirit, Creator Come', and the procession came solemnly in.

As far as the altar boys were concerned, it wasn't a procession so much as a race, which, needless to say, they won by half a length – of the church, the archbishop and chaplain trailing badly behind. In fact, they took so long to reach the sanctuary that we ran out of verses and had to sing the hymn three times over. All eyes were glued on the archbishop, wondering if he'd reach the altar safely. He did, as it happens, but it was touch and go. One thing is certain: he'd never have succeeded without his long staff.

His safe arrival at the altar was our cue to sit down, which everybody did with relief, including the archbishop, and Mass started. Shortly after, he began to address the congregation. In those days, a bishop's address at Confirmation had little to do with the service; it was meant for a wider audience and usually made the newspapers. Only near its end would it involve the congregation. But I doubt if I'd have been interested anyway,

154

between one thing and another. I mean to say, what with me being so far from the altar, and the bishop being so feeble and probably out of puff after his long walk up the centre of the church, I couldn't for the life of me catch a word of his address. Every now and then I stretched my neck to have a look, but there he was, going on and on, with no end in sight. It was at times like this that my mind wandered, and as it happened, I began thinking of Brother George.

Of all the Brothers in our school he was the most popular, except when he was in one of his moods. Then woe betide you if you fell victim to his tongue, for he could be very sarcastic – in fact, his sarcasm was a far more effective weapon than his strap. I'd seen senior boys, sixteen-year-olds – young men, you might say – reduced to tears by a telling-off from Brother George. Fortunately, his bad moods were rare enough, but we had to be on constant alert for the well-known signs. Unlike Goldsmith's *'boding tremblers who learned to trace/The day's disasters in his morning face'*, we could trace disaster, not in Brother George's face, but in his hair. He had none on top, and to disguise his baldness he carefully cultivated some long wisps of hair that grew over one ear. These he kept brushed across the top of his head, where they remained pat when all was calm. When he was agitated and disturbed, however, they took unto themselves a life of their own, and kept falling over his forehead, to be swept back in place again by his hand. The angrier he became, the more often he had to brush the hair out of his eyes.

Willie Morrison and I had talked about this very thing. As usual, he had a scientific explanation. He said, 'It's a phenomnion – '

'A wot?'

' – caused by a thing called "ecstatic electricity". Ah ye know, everyone has it on their bodies, only some have more of it than others.'

'I see what ye mean,' I said. 'Like freckles.'

As I looked up at Brother George in Monkstown parish church, I was delighted to see that his hair was in place and everything was all right.

Well, all good things come to an end, as they say, and that's also true about bishops' homilies. Under cover of the racket of everyone kneeling down again, Spuggy said to me, 'You know you're after takin' the Pledge, don't you?'

'Get away!' I said. 'I took nothing.'

'We all took it. Everyone answered the bishop and made the promise. The Pledge means that we won't be able to take a jar as long as we live.'

'It doesn't count for me,' I said smugly, "cos I couldn't hear a word the bishop said. I took nothin', I tell ye.'

'Wouldya believe it?' hissed Lee in front of me. 'Don't some fellas have all the luck?'

At a certain point of the Mass the bishop, steadied by the chaplain, made his way down to the front row of boys to begin the Confirmations. My pulse began to race, even though I knew I had tucks of time yet for mental revision of the Catechism.

It was in the days of the long catechism, and as I said before, you had to be word perfect, it was no good only getting the gist of it. The compilers knew how to scatter hidden traps and pitfalls among the questions, which were deliberately designed to trap you. The long catechism was a minefield, and no boy could safely get through it without a scratch, not even Willie Morrison. On top of that, it was full of mysterious phrases like 'forbidden degrees of kindred' which we rattled off by rote, not understanding what on earth they meant. And they weren't the only things we didn't understand. For instance, it said that mysteries like the Blessed Trinity were 'beyond our comprehension'.

'Do you know, Dunne,' the Master asked me, 'what is meant by "beyond our comprehension"?'

'Please sir, I . . . I don't understand . . . ' I faltered.

'Exactly,' he said, leaving me none the wiser.

From the Catechism I heard of sins I never knew existed, like 'calumny and detraction', 'lust', 'sloth', and one called 'covetousness'. Only for the Catechism, I wouldn't have heard of them.

'Wouldn't it be great gas confessin' some of them to Father Burke in the box,' I was thinking. 'It'd be somethin' to tell him anyway. Yeah, I'd fancy confessin' the sin of "sloth"; I like the sound o' that one. It reminds me of something slimy, like a snail. But what if he asked me about it? Better not chance it. Then there's what the Catechism calls "sins of the flesh", although it doesn't go into any details. What about tellin' a few of them? Wonder what they are, anyway. Eatin' "flesh meat" on a Friday, I suppose. On second thoughts, no use confessin' them . . . fat chance of committin' them anyway, because I only eat what I get, and we never get meat on Friday, as Father Burke well knows.'

After a while I gave up thinking about the Catechism and all its mysteries. I decided instead to trust to luck, because 'At this stage,' I said to myself, 'it's too late to do anything about it.'

I stretched my neck to see how the bishop was getting on. 'My God, he's only halfway down,' I thought. 'At the rate he's goin' I'll have four grandchildren an' a beard down to me belly button by the time he gets to me.'

Not surprisingly, the old mind began to wander again, and I was thinking, 'Why is it that when I'm asked a question in school I have two problems: at what point to begin my answer, and when to finish? (If I don't know the answer, of course, I have only one.) And while gathering my wits in search of a starting point, I hum and haw by saying, "Well, you see sir, it was like this", at which point the teacher usually says, "and don't make a meal of it" or "and spare us from one of your usual lectures, if you please." The last three words are drawn out for greater effect, and usually cause a titter around me . . . I won't have any such problems today, for there's no scope at all in the Catechism for makey-up answers . . . '

And so it went on, until suddenly there was the bishop sliding into the seat right in front of me. I couldn't believe my eyes. How on earth I failed to notice him coming is a mystery that will haunt me forever. So unexpected was his arrival that he must have sprung up through a crack in the floor. That's the only explanation I can think of. One minute I thought he was far up the church, the next he was on top of me. Here was my moment of truth. Without any introduction, formality, pre-amble or anything, he asked, 'Who is Jesus Christ?'

Now, the prescribed answer was one of the three simplest ones in the whole of the Catechism: 'Jesus Christ is God and the second Person of the Blessed Trinity.' No hidden traps, no jaw-breakers, no mysterious phrases. In fact, a puddin'. But taken off guard as I was, and in shock, I never associated the question with the Catechism, but treated it as an informal enquiry, though it did strike me as an odd question coming from a bis-hop.

'Jesus Christ?' I said. 'Well you see, my lordship, it was like this . . . ' and I launched into my own version of the life of Christ. I decided I'd begin with His birth in the stable at Bethlehem, and so, imitating Sister Victor of my convent days, I told him about the star in the east, the shepherds on the hills, the bit about 'no room at the inn', the three wise kings, and when I was halfway through the slaughter of the Holy Innocents I had to pull up in a screech of brakes, for clearly there was some-thing the matter with the bishop. I noticed Father Burke giving an indulgent smile, so I guessed that the bishop was amused – or perhaps doing his best to keep from laughing. If so, he was not succeeding very well. Can you imagine this ancient bishop actually laughing in church? Laughing in the middle of Con-firmation! I can tell you now that laughing in church in 1936 was unheard of, and bordered on the sacrilegious. But for a bis-hop to do it! Nor was it a pretty sight: his body trembled from head to toe; his pale face flushed to a vivid red, then purple, then pink. Eyes tightly closed, lips pursed and twisted, he looked like a bishop who had just taken a generous slurp from an extra-sour lemon and was looking for somewhere to spit. I stood goggle-eyed.

Just then, frantic activity in the side aisle tore my attention away from the bishop. Brother George's hair was doing the Haymakers' Jig, and he was flapping his hands up and down, trying to control it. But for the complete absence of rhythm in the hand-movements, he'd have resembled the bandmaster conducting a spirited rendition of a Sousa march. The best description is of a bookmaker's tout tick-tacking the odds to someone up in the gallery.

When the bishop finally subsided, he asked me my name. 'Wi-Wi-William, my lordship,' I stammered. This drew from the Brother a long hissing intake of breath, the like of which you can hear in the shoemakers' shop when a fella hits his thumb with the hammer.

The chaplain bent to the bishop's ear and in a stage whisper that must have been heard up the other end of the church told him my name wasn't William at all, but Joseph.

'Well, Joseph – or William,' said the bishop, beginning to shake again, as though about to give a repeat performance, 'you'll go far.'

I was in such a daze that I remember little of the rest of my Confirmation, and that only vaguely. I was thinking that now I'd surely blown my chance of capturing the sixpence prize promised to the boy who was best in his catechism test. (I wouldn't mind, only I had my heart set on buying a kite.)

It was Spuggy's turn to be confirmed next, and I was amazed to hear that he'd taken 'Jarlath' for his Confirmation name. 'What's the matter with Spuggy?' I was thinking. 'Where's he goin' with his "Jarlath"? He's not a bit like a Jarlath.' Some lads had actually laughed when they heard that I was taking a name as ordinary as William (my dad's name), most of them going for unusual names, and boy were there some beauties! There was a plethora of Aloysiuses, Ignatius Loyolas, Bonaventures and Sebastians, but only a few Patricks, Josephs and Johns. A lad from Kilkenny took Gerard-Majella (imagine!), because a picture of the saint had hung over his bed. Another lad took Pancratius, after a Christian eaten by lions in Rome in the olden days. The story about that was in our English reader, and was probably made up, I shouldn't wonder.

But if Jarlath surprised me for Spuggy, I was dumbfounded when Ape's turn came. When I heard Ape's new name, it was all I could do to stop myself from splashing out laughing. '"*Cedric*",' said I in disbelief. 'I mean to say . . . "Cedric"!' Now, had it been Max, after Max Baer the boxer . . . I looked beyond Spuggy towards Ape, and by coincidence our eyes met. His glared at mine from under a frown; mine reassured his with a smile, as though to say: 'Don't worry oul' son, yer secret is safe with me. Ye've nothin' to worry about – nothin' at all. Sure who'd be brave enough to call *you* Cedric?' After all, he wasn't called Ape for nothing.

The Confirmations ended with the Wynne twins. Con was the side drummer in our band and Charlie played solo cornet, and when I tell you that a sweeter cornet was not to be heard throughout the length and breadth of Ireland, it's no lie. Why, you'd cheerfully get up before the lark on a frosty morning to hear Charlie play 'Just a Song at Twilight' on his cornet – not that he'd be playing it so early anyway; I'm only saying . . . And as for his bugle-calls – especially the one for dinner: 'Come to the Cook-house Door, Boys' – why that must be the sweetest bugle-call I ever heard in my whole life, the way Charlie blew it.

Anyhow, we all watched the bishop shuffle up the aisle again to the altar, our eyes following him all the way, wondering if he'd make it the second time round. But he did.

After Benediction we stood up for the final hymn, whose last chord didn't have time to echo from the rafters before I headed a stampede for the door in a way that was sure to earn us a stiff telling-off later on. But I didn't care. I had to get away from the place that had witnessed my greatest humiliation. We congregated outside, and welcome though the sunshine and fresh air were, I buried myself among the other lads like a chicken under its mother's wing, fearful of what the Brother would say. Then, figuring that he could hardly do much in so public a place, I decided to get it over with as soon as possible.

I ventured my head 'over the top' as they say, and saw him at once at the far edge of the crowd, now swollen by the addition of parents and families plus the rest of the boys from our school. Would you believe it, didn't he spot me at that very moment? Taking the shortest distance between two points, he ploughed his way in my direction. I admired the expert way he cut a swathe through the dense crowd, his only incentive being to confront me. As I watched, I thought that the Antarctic explorer Sir Ernest Shackleton could have done with Brother George among his crew when his ship got stuck in the pack ice – he'd have had it free in no time.

Without a word, he glared down on me for what seemed like several minutes. A stranger happening along just then might be pardoned for thinking that the Brother was at a loss for words. Not one bit! This inaction, this silent survey, this arm-folded, sloped-back stance was a part of the Brother's tactics, specially designed to fray the victim's nerves to shreds. And how successful it was in my case! He looked awesome, taller (perhaps I was cringing?), his hat jammed far down on his head, its brim nearly touching the bridge of his nose (another bad sign, proof that it had been donned when he was in a bad mood). At last the axe fell. For the benefit of all and sundry, he asked, 'What do you think of a *clown* who couldn't answer the simplest question in the whole of the Catechism and, if you don't mind, not only that, but doesn't he then go and forget his own name?'

From my erstwhile friends there flowed guffaws of servile laughter which delighted the Brother. Thus encouraged, he tapped the toe of one foot softly on the ground (his way of showing that he was the very quintessence of patience) and hissed, 'Well, Professor, what interesting explanation have you got for us this time? And pray, preserve us from one of your usual lectures, if you please.' More titters and sniggers.

'I was thinking: '"Professor", he called me. I hope I'm not goin' to be stuck with that tag for the rest o' me life.'

'Proceed, if you don't mind,' he said impatiently. 'We'd all like to hear from you today, unless you happen to have a more pressing engagement.'

'Well, you see sir, it was like this,' I replied, deciding to kick the Catechism question over the sideline. 'I thought the bishop wanted to know my Confirmation name, which is William.'

'And what, pray, did the bishop say to you?'

'Sir, he didn't seem to mind at all.'

'But what did he say exactly? I didn't hear.'

'Sir, he told me I'll go far.'

'You'll go far?'

'Yes, sir.' He joined his hands and with face raised piously to heaven, fervently prayed: 'Please, oh God, *please make it soon.*' There was a sprinkling of 'Amen's among the laughter.

19

HOLIDAYS

Those who had relatives to claim them were allowed home for three days in the first week of August, and the same at Christmas.

I was appalled to see where my mother, stepfather and baby half-sister Maura lived. It consisted of a tiny 'back parlour' of a tenement house in James' Street, Dublin – dark, unbelievably dingy and gloomy, and so packed with furniture that I had to shuffle sideways when moving within its cluttered confines.

The furniture came from an era when heavy and substantial were essential qualities in its manufacture. Two beds, double and single, placed like an inverted T, two sideboards with a few gewgaws on top, a round table and six mahogany chairs with red upholstered seats, a couple of bentwood kitchen chairs and a floor-to-ceiling glass display cabinet of polished mahogany: that was the furniture the room contained. The cabinet was empty; the silver and porcelain ornaments that had once graced its shelves were long since sold or pawned. Patrick, my stepfather, had drained everything my father had left to my mother, and had brought her to this sorry level.

There was no electricity laid on, and Mother, to eke out the gas, delayed lighting the single gas mantle as long as possible in the evening – that is, until my stepfather complained that he couldn't see the list of runners in the paper. A paraffin oil lamp served as standby against the not-infrequent times when Mother hadn't got a penny to insert in the gas meter. A small fireplace and range occupied the angle of one corner of the room, for heat only, because it was cheaper to cook on a black-leaded cast-iron gas cooker.

The room's only sash window overlooked a small yard,

whose ten-foot wall prevented the sunlight from reaching us. A water tap and outside flush lavatory served the tenement's three families, two downstairs and one up. To prevent the other tenants from 'spying' in on us from the yard, multi-coloured paper had been pasted over the bottom half of our heavily draped window, further reducing the room's scanty natural lighting. From the gale-force wind forever blowing through the house between the permanently open front and back doors, a cold draught filtered under our door, providing more than enough ventilation. It did little, however, to abate the breath-catching smell of paraffin oil which impregnated everything and took over the room as only paraffin oil can do. Even the food tasted of it.

Massive mirrors almost completely covered three walls, and gave false additional dimensions to the room, their heavy gilt frames beautifully ornamented at each corner by cherubs, and at the top of the frame stood a large eagle with wings out-stretched. These mirrors, and the heavy mahogany furniture, were what Mother called 'relics of old decency, from when your poor daddy was alive.' On the small sections of the walls not hidden by the mirrors hung three beautifully carved maho-gany clocks which hadn't worked for years. Mother steadfastly refused to part with a single surplus item, and obstinately clung to the hope that some day she would have her own house again.

My stepfather (I could never bring myself to call him Dad) was the 'Uncle' Patrick of my tender years. He had a deep jea-lousy of my father's memory, and not surprisingly any men-tion of Dad in his presence was strictly avoided in the interests of peace. As a result, I never managed to learn anything from Mother about my father, so that to this day I have nothing but a vague outline of him. Patrick destroyed any photographs of him, except one, which mother somehow managed to salvage, but not before it had been folded down its centre in such a way that the crease and tiny cracks all but obliterated the face. I have it still.

My stepfather never worked in his life, and boasted of that fact, adding that he was 'independent, and would never become another man's slave'. His sole income was one pound a week disability pension from the Great War, and yet in spite of his disability, about which he was always very reticent, he enjoyed perfect health. At an early stage in the war he had seriously overstayed his leave, and so vigilant were the military police of the day – so active on the trail of deserters – that life on the run for Patrick became too uncomfortable.

Figuring correctly that the last place the military would search for him was in the army itself, he re-enlisted in the name of Patrick O'Neill instead of his own name, Patrick Conway. As Private O'Neill, he served throughout the remainder of the war, and under that name he applied for, and was granted, a disability pension when the war was over.

He was a young man then, and single, and a pound a week – even in those days – was not enough to live on: nor was it intended to be. Most other pensioners treated it as a supplement to another wage, or the dole if they were unemployed, but Patrick was not like that. He would not look for a job in case the British Pensions Board got wind of it and raised questions about his 'disability', concerning which there was something of a mystery anyway. He claimed he had a weak back. To protect his pension, he didn't sign on at the Labour Exchange or draw the dole, for he would then have been obliged to accept whatever job might be offered. Besides, the dole didn't accord with his principles of independence.

In 1929 he married my mother (within a year of Una's and my being sent away), at which stage he should have notified the British Pensions Board of his marital status and claimed the higher rate of pension. But as a copy of his marriage certificate would have had to accompany the application, of course, his true identity would have come to light, as would the 'absence without leave' episode of his army service. So any action on his part would probably have jeopardised the very pension itself, and since Patrick was not prepared to take such a risk, he had no option, as he saw it, but to draw the pension under a false name, at the single man's rate – and to remain unemployed. It didn't bother him in the slightest that in doing this he was imposing a life of poverty and utter misery on his wife.

Of course, I didn't learn any of this until long after I had left school, but I saw those appalling living conditions when I came home on my short holidays and had to share them. I saw Mother's plight as Patrick's wife when he gradually revealed himself in his true colours. Yes, Patrick was difficult to live with and hard to please, especially about his food, and since he was completely toothless, Mother worried to distraction at dinnertime about the meat, hoping to God it would be tender enough for him, and that he would manage to chew it with his gums. He shouted and raged and swore when things weren't to his liking. Nor was it solely the food's quality that Mother worried about; no, she often went without food herself in seeing that Patrick had enough to eat. When I came home for good, the war was on. Certain foods were rationed – tea most of all – yet he took the family's tea rations for himself, leaving us to make do with shell cocoa. Mother would whisper to me, 'Humour him, Joe, for peace's sake. Please.'

Patrick was slight of build, 'of the greyhound breed', as he said himself. His deep-set, piercing black eyes stared out from a shrunken, toothless face. He stayed in all day 'studying form' in the newspaper and picking his fancies, which he wrote in pencil with great difficulty, in block capitals, on small betting slips. These he called 'each-way accumulators'. There might be five or six horses on the list. He also had shorter lists called 'sixpence-each-way up-an'-down trebles', and only an expert could figure out how they worked.

The trouble was that he expected Mother to listen attentively while he talked and talked all day about his selections and about his hard luck in the previous venture. She became almost demented. Seldom if ever did he win anything back (despite a most careful study of forms before making his final selection). Mother's constant fear was that he might win, but whenever he did, it was only a few shillings. Needless to say, his winnings went on beer. This invariably spelt trouble for Mother, because sober, Patrick was a garrulous bore – drunk, a truculent bully. It was not until I came home from school for good that I saw more and more of this side of his character.

Fortunately for Mother's peace of mind, Patrick lost his bets most of the time, but losing never discouraged him from talking about them. Indeed, the reverse was the case, for his hard-luck stories were legion: how he changed his betting slip at the last minute and would have won a fortune if he had left it alone. 'I met a gobshite in the bookie's who persuaded me that Subtle Serpent [he pronounced it 'subtile'] was past the post, an' I changed me docket the last minit.' Or he'd say, 'I'd four up in an accumulator and the fifth one was only bet [beaten] by a snot.'

As though the subject of horses was not enough to bore Mother to death's door, there were the Sunday newspaper competitions as well – the *Independent* and *Chronicle* crossword competitions, and the *Sunday Dispatch* 'Pick the First Three Horses'. He always claimed to have been only one step away from the top prize. It was a case of 'Wait till ye hear the hard luck I had this week.' And so he spent his life, 'working' at the horses and newspaper competitions with the stub of a pencil, smoking his pipe, and spitting into the fire. And talking about them non-stop! The last thing we heard before going to sleep at night was Patrick's voice droning on and on. He sat up in bed, still wearing his hat, still smoking his pipe. (Whatever might go short in the house, it wasn't pipe tobacco.)

Wednesday was a special day, the day Patrick went to Usher's Quay post office on the banks of the Liffey to draw his pension. He walked – or rather marched – everywhere with the bearing of a soldier: head erect, chest out, arms swinging, trousers neatly pressed, brown shoes shining. He was 'on parade' for the neighbours' inspection.

He had prepared for this hours before. While polishing his shoes with Kiwi polish (oxblood colour), he waffled on about the amount of bull's blood that went into the making of it. His trousers, carefully placed under the mattress the night before, were now withdrawn perfectly pressed. Then came the ritual of brushing his felt hat, sitting on the side of the bed, the only time when his completely bald bullet-head was uncovered. A long-drawn-out operation this, one to savour and enjoy. To the rhythmic strokes of the clothes-brush he gave his rapt attention, applying exactly the right pressure to exactly the right spot. It was a loving, sensual experience, definitely not one to be rushed. Again and again he explained the importance of 'brushin' with the grain', and as for returning his hat to his head later, sure that was an art in itself, repeated again and again – slowly, carefully – until he was satisfied that the hat inclined at just the right angle, 'tilted towards the Kildare side' – whatever that meant. The various procedures involved in getting ready to collect his pension occupied several hours, and were repeatedly checked in the mirrors. And why not? Not since the previous Wednesday had he been exposed to public view. He gave up going to church on Sunday because it meant he had to remove his hat in public. Like an actor in the wings, afraid to go on stage, Patrick withdrew from the very door again and again for one excuse or another. 'I've a feelin' I'm forgettin' something' or 'Have you any message for Maggie?' he'd say. In sheer desperation Mother would raise her eyes to heaven, like a saint in a holy picture, and say, 'Will you for God's sake lose yourself.' It sounded like a prayer from the heart.

After the post office, Patrick's next port of call was Aunt Maggie's house. He called in without fail every Wednesday at Aunt Maggie's bidding, an obligation to be met under pain of mortal sin. She sweetened the visit with half a crown and some-times half an ounce of 'twist' pipe tobacco as well, so called be-cause it was cut from a large coil. He was her brother, she re-garded him as the wayward member of her family, and this was her way of keeping tabs on him. He called, more for the money she gave 'for himself' than for love of her. After a decent interval he was off to the bookies in time for the first race, and there he dallied until the last results of the day came in.

Aunt Maggie was large and domineering, a shrewish, overbearing, bossy woman, or 'targer', as Patrick called her behind her back. Everyone quaked in her presence, but she was the only one who was a match for Patrick. Her first marriage had been to Uncle Frank, my mother's brother, who died young ('A merciful release,' Mother said). She kept a small dog, a Pomeranian, whose vicious snapping and snarling put the fear of God into small boys and sent large mastiffs scurrying away with their tail between their legs. She lived in a cottage in South Summer Street, one of a terrace which Jacobs, the biscuit people, rented to some of their employees. Her husband, Uncle Jim, was a fitter in the Jacobs Peter Street factory, and was 'on call' after hours. She was house-proud and kept the place spotless; there was not a pin astray. Patrick said it was 'a brave speck of dust that would land on anything Maggie owned.' He was afraid to touch anything on his visits, or even to sit down, for fear of ruffling a cushion. She let him smoke his pipe though – even encouraged him with the odd half-ounce of twist – but it was more than his life was worth to spit into her fire. For the rest of the day he complained bitterly of 'the heart burd'n after havin' to swally all me spits in Maggie's' and vowed solemnly never to go again.

There was a big hooley in Aunt Maggie's every year, the day after Christmas Day, and the little house was full to bursting with relations. A separate sitting for tea was reserved for the children, before the grown-ups sat down to theirs. The table was a feast for the eye as well as for the palate – dish upon dish of mince pies, plum pudding, jam tarts and apple tarts, and fancy cakes in abundance, all laid out in a mouth-watering display. But let any child's hand wander towards a cake and Aunt Maggie, standing over us with arms folded, boomed out: 'There's plenty o' bread an' buther there now for yez.' At once the errant hand was drawn back to the plainer fare, for the threat behind the announcement was unmistakable. And so we children rose from the table after a while, stuffed to the gills with bread and butter, not having had a taste of even one of the still mouth-watering goodies.

20

Dublin in the 1930s

It was a great advantage to be born, as it were, at the age of eleven: to burst upon the city suddenly, instead of getting to know it gradually from infancy like everyone else. Consequently, when I came home for three days in August and at Christmas, I instinctively observed everything with sharper interest than did 'outside boys' of a similar age. What were to them ordinary, run-of-the-mill sights were to me of absorbing interest, and I mentally noted everything in order to describe things to my schoolmates later.

My short holidays went on formal visits to aunts and uncles, accompanied by my mother – much as nowadays children are taken to see relations and family friends on special occasions like First Holy Communion and Confirmation days. Gifts of money were slipped into my hand – sixpence, or a shilling – so that in a few days I had a pound in my pocket. It was a small fortune to a child, for in those days it took two hundred and forty pennies to make a pound, each penny was worth four farthings, and you could buy enough sweets for a farthing to share with a pal or two. I had relations (using the word loosely) in Inchicore, South Earl Street, South Summer Street, Gray Street, Heytesbury Street, Mountjoy Street, Temple Bar and Marino, and Mother brought me to see them on foot (not all on the same day, of course). We walked because she regarded the tram as an unnecessary luxury, and it suited me too. Taking the tram was a waste of money, even though it was cheap – a tuppenny fare got one from terminus to terminus on most routes in the city, which in those days extended only little beyond the Royal Canal and North Circular Road on the north side, and the Grand Canal on the south.

Dublin then had an unenviable reputation for its large slum areas. Probably most of its population in the 1930s lived in tenement houses, sad wrecks that had once been posh 'town-houses' of the gentry in former centuries. They had no bath-rooms, and three or four families had to share a single tap and outside lavatory. Cooking and lighting were by gas, there being no electricity. Radios were battery-operated, though many families were without one. By comparison, people fortunate enough to have a house to themselves, even to rent, were considered com-fortably off – a few steps up the social ladder. The relations and friends we visited were in that category, and as I sat on the edge of a chair in an aunt's parlour I observed every detail of the house – pictures, furniture, ornaments. While the adults talked, I looked about me, noting everything. I had so many aunts I had trouble identifying them outside their home when Mother and I went shopping, so I associated each in my mind with some feature of her house.

'Who was that you were talking to?' I'd ask.

'That was your Aunt Bridge.'

'Is Aunt Bridge the auntie who has the picture of Grattan's parliament hanging in the hall?'

'No, that's Aunt Cissie.'

'Well, is she the one with the canary then?'

'No, that's Aunt Mary Kate.'

'Well, who is she then?'

'She lives in Temple Bar. You know, beside the Liffey.'

This confusion arose because I wasn't home long enough to know my aunts properly. When I returned to school, my stories about my 'rich relations' lost nothing in the telling. 'They have a goose and ham for dinner every Christmas, do you know that?' I boasted. 'Just imagine a whole ham and goose or turkey gawking down at you from the middle of their sideboard. They have electric light too, and a wireless of their very own, an' lis-ten to this: some even have a pianna, believe it or not.'

The piano held pride of place in the parlour (a front room kept locked and out of bounds to all but the mother of the family, so as to be spotlessly clean and presentable for any visitors who might call). If no member of the family could play the piano, so what; it was purchased nonetheless as an expensive piece of furniture. It was more than that, though: it was a status symbol too, and came to life whenever a hooley was thrown, for it would be a poor hooley indeed where no one could be found to play it. Hooleys were parties: gatherings of friends and relations for tea, drinking and singing, not necessarily in that order, starting early in the evening and continuing into the small hours of the following day. Hooleys were 'thrown', never held, to celebrate an event like Christmas, a wedding engagement, or a visit home from England of a son or daughter – or sometimes for no reason. Houses were small, and seldom had enough room for dancing. Neighbours were invited too, since they were going to have a sleepless night anyway. Liquid refreshments were the prominent feature of every hooley, the guests' needs in that regard being the host's responsibility, not his wife's. The main source of supply came from kegs of Guinness – two at least – in the backyard or garden, and the local publican helped out with a present of a bottle of port and a loan of drinking glasses, since the host was usually a regular customer. One of the guests acted as Master of Ceremonies, and it was his function to regulate the entertainment by calling on the guests in turn for a song or party piece, usually contributed after an unconvincing expression of modest reluctance, a kind of formality that had to be gone through first. 'Very well then, I'll sing if there's nobody else . . . I'm sufferin' from the divil's own cold, I'll have you know, so I won't be at me best, I hope yez don't mind . . . ' or, 'I'm really not a singer at all, I only sing in the bath, an' don't get much practice.'

'Go 'long outa that with ye, ye've a lovely voice. What about "Sweet Spirit Hear me Prayer"?'

'Aw, I'm past that one now.'

'Well I'll ask someone else then.'

'Oh very well, all right so, I'll sing, but don't say I didn't warn yez.'

My mother was always called upon to contribute, for she had a lovely voice. 'Whisht everyone, Aunt Nellie is goin' to sing.' This was relayed to the back room, and was followed by a gradual hush. Her favourite was 'After the Ball Was Over', followed by 'I Dreamt I Dwelt' from *The Bohemian Girl*. She sang in a posh voice.

Most of the songs popular in the 1930s were forty-year-old music-hall hits from the 'Gay Nineties' or songs that had come out during the Great War. It was at the hooleys that I first heard the words of songs we played in the school band, words that were obliterated from our band parts as unsuitable for us, owing to their love motif.

The front room or parlour in a house was a cold room, the fire being lit only when special visitors came. Before central heating was heard of in private houses, only one room was kept warm and that was where the family sat most of the day. It was called the 'living room' for that reason, and it was where they dined too. Even in the coldest weather the fire was not lit elsewhere in the house, not even in a bedroom, unless a member of the family fell ill. As a general rule the beds were warmed an hour or so before bedtime by placing a hot-water jar or bottle between the sheets, or the clothes iron was heated on the gas hob, wrapped in a cloth and inserted in the bed. Cold houses forced people to dress in warmer clothes, and it was not at all uncommon for a man to keep his hat or cap on all the time indoors, even during meals, especially if he was bald. When out of doors, women wore hats or shawls and men rarely went about without a hat or cap.

One or two of my aunts owned a gramophone, which was kept in the parlour and 'put on' to entertain special visitors. The records included Jimmy O'Dea's, who was then all the rage, and also tunes dating from the turn of the century, for songs endured longer than the present-day pops. As well as playing the records, my aunt wound up the gramophone with a handle inserted in the side, and changed the steel needle when the sound became scratchy. It was the woman's job to see to the entertainment, as well as tea and eatables; the man's, to 'look after' the stronger refreshments for the visitors – under his wife's supervision, of course. 'Look after Mr Conway there, can't ye see his glass is nearly gone dhry.' It was 'manners' for guests to make a modest attempt at declining another drink, taking care not to overdo it lest they be taken at their word. Everyone understood these formalities, even the host, and they were observed for politeness' sake. Tea was a formal 'sit-down-to' affair in the living room, and the best delph from the display cabinet or 'glass-case' was used. Supper was a cup of tea and a plate in the hand, taken in the parlour.

For Christmas dinner Mother bought a pig's cheek or a piece of bacon in Thomas Street, having saved all the year in 'Flana-gan's Christmas "Diddley" Club' in James' Street. She also bought a Dundee cake and the ingredients of a plum pudding. After thoroughly mixing the pudding with her hands in a large basin, she boiled it for a whole day in a cloth, the steam causing the wallpaper to come out in large bubbles. Then she hung it from a hook in the ceiling for a week or two 'to mature'. My mother's Christmas pudding was the spiciest I ever tasted, and repeated for the day, like cod-liver oil.

Thomas Street was hugely popular as a market place, at-tracting shoppers from all over the city. It was said to have a 'money side' and a 'sunny side'. The former consisted entirely of shops – dairies, grocers, butchers, hardware stores – and two large department stores, Frawley's and Dufly's, all doing a thriving business. The opposite side was occupied for the most part by Blanchardstown Mills, the Irish Agricultural Whole-sale Society, Saint Augustine's Priory and the church known as John's Lane Church. There were one or two small, family-run shops on that side also, but these gave the appearance of having a hard struggle just to stay open. Some years later Woolworths opened a branch on the 'sunny side' and people thought that *that* would surely inject life into it at last, but it made no dif-ference, for after only a few years Woolworths had to admit defeat and close its shutters. Inexplicably, shoppers wouldn't cross the street.

The contrast between the two sides of the street was extra-ordinary – the one noisy and bustling with business, the other quietly snoozing in the sun like a Spanish village at siesta. Thomas Street's 'money side' boasted branches of Dublin's top grocery chainstores of the day: Lipton's, Home & Colonial, Bacon Shops, Caesars' Butchers, Payantakes and also the May-pole Dairies. Business went on at a roaring rate until well past ten every night, all year round.

Following well-established tradition, grocers gave their regular customers a Christmas present, usually an iced cake or a tin of biscuits. Butchers gave a giant red candle. And they knew every customer personally, for business was on a personal basis, each customer a special one. It was common practice for the grocer and the assistants to ask after a customer's family, and to comment in a way that would be resented today and seen as an intrusion on one's privacy – this while the butter was slapped into neat shapes with ridged wooden spatulas dipped in water, or while the purchases were being wrapped neatly in brown-paper parcels and tied securely with white twine. And while that was going on, other customers stood by listening unashamedly as they waited to be served.

'And isn't it six you have in the family, Mrs Burd'n? Seven? Be the hokey! All keepin' well I hope? Ah yes . . . Good, good . . . Mary's your eldest, isn't that right? She'd be how old now? Fourteen, is it? My blesses, a young lady, ye might say. But isn't time flyin'! Say hello to Himself for me, won't yeh? Keepin' well too, is 'e? Good, good. Still workin' in the Distillery, isn't he? Good, good. An' more *Power* to his elbow, if ye'll pard'n me little joke. There y'are now, Mrs Burd'n, an' here's a little some-thing for yerself as well, an' a Merry Christmas to go with it, ma'am. Yes, Mrs Conway, an' how're *you* keepin'? . . . Good, good. An' what can I be gettin' ye?'

On the same side of the street, just off the footpath and stretching to the corner of Francis Street, stood a line of women dealers known as 'shawlies', from the black woollen shawl in which they wrapped themselves in all weathers. Each shawlie had a stall consisting of a deep, chest-high wooden barrow on three wheels, and across its top a baker's bread-board to serve as a counter on which the fruit and vegetables were displayed. They were family businesses these, each barrow handed down from mother to daughter for generations, along with the 'claim' to the site or pitch. It was the women who ran those businesses – never the husbands. The shawlies maintained a friendly though keen competition with one another and shouted out their wares in strident voices to attract the passers-by, so between them and the busy motor and horse-drawn traffic the air was vibrant with sound.

The famous Mushatt's chemist's shop stood in Francis Street opposite the Tivoli Cinema, just around the corner from Thomas Street. Everything sold there was 'made up' by Mr Mushatt himself, and customers came from all over the city for his brands of skin- or eye-ointments, as well as for lotions and potions, and 'bottles' for every imaginable complaint. Posted in the window was an advertisement saying: 'We Dispense with Accuracy', for Mr Mushatt had a great sense of humour. A 'Mullingar man' he was, by all accounts, though it seemed to me he must have hailed from India, judging by his colour and accent. There's a story told about a lady asking Mr Mushatt for Epsom salts.

'Sorry. We don't stock the common proprietary brands here, ma'am, only our own special makes,' he told her. 'I'm surprised you don't know that already. However, I can let you have this (holding up a packet), which we call "Morning Salts".'

'What's the difference between that and Epsom Salts?' the lady wanted to know.

'About a minute and a half,' was the reply.

In the 1930s, chemists made up and dispensed all their prescriptions themselves, a job done nowadays by the manufacturers, who supply everything pre-packaged or bottled. You could smell a chemist's shop fifty yards away – a mixture of chemical and medicine odours – and at night you would see lights shining on the cobbled street outside, beamed through three large carboys, globular glass containers in red, blue and green that were placed in the window, which were a chemist's trademark.

Mother met a lot of friends out shopping in Thomas Street, and they'd stand talking for ages about people in the locality who were ill, or were getting married, or having babies. Her friends would press a thrupenny bit or a tanner (sixpence) into my hand to 'get some sweets for yerself' and I was often the richer by a bob or two.

We hailed from this area originally – in fact, I was born in number 39 Reginald Street, only four or five doors from the Coombe and a few hundred yards from Thomas Street, so Mother was well known and popular. The Liberties was like a town within a city, whose people were as one huge happy family, renowned for friendliness and wit. Years after leaving school, I would see Mother scanning the *Evening Mail*'s death columns to see if any of 'the old stock', as she fondly called them, were mentioned, and she returned there for many a wake and a reunion with some old friends of long ago, with whom she chatted away the night while keeping vigil over the departed one.

Thanks to Mother's generous relations and friends whom I met on my brief holidays from school, I could treat her to seats in the gods in the Olympia Theatre to see Jimmy O'Dea's Christmas pantomime, and his August show too. It was overshadowed by my having to return to school next day. I looked wistfully at the happy, laughing audience, and with special envy at boys my own age. But the sadness dissipated soon in the atmosphere of the theatre.

I persuaded Mother to take what money I had left over, and eventually she gave in, saying, 'Mind you, it's only a loan now, remember that.' She would compromise by buying sweets and ginger cake for me to take back to school. No matter how hard I tried to hold back my tears, parting was a sorrowful occasion, for Mother too. It upset me to think of her living in the awful squalor of that dismal tenement room she called home, and I determined some day to get her the house of her own for which she longed so much. I am glad to say that eventually I managed to do so, in a way that I will relate later.

21

My Acting Career

Earlier, I mentioned that Willie Redmond, the bandmaster, produced plays and musical revues in the recreation hall. It was my misfortune to get a part in a play, and Willie's misfortune too. It was called *The Confidential Clerk*, or maybe *The Private Secretary*, I'm not sure. I don't recall much of the plot, either, but I do remember that the setting was a country house in Victorian England, and that I was a university student. There was no dress rehearsal as such, because – except for one or two players – we wore our own clothes. Arthur Cluffe played the Colonel, for which role he borrowed a suit of clothes a few sizes too large, and inside his waistcoat and trousers he stuffed a large pillow or cushion to give himself a fine paunch. He also wore a walrus moustache.

The fellow in the title role had to dress as a Protestant clergyman – why, I couldn't for the life of me figure out, because the part had no religious or church connections that I could see. The nearest the producer could go to meeting the costume requirement in his case was to borrow a Christian Brother's outdoor suit and collar.

There was one performance only and naturally the full school attended, the Community of Brothers occupying the front row of seats to be sure of missing nothing. I was nearly sick from nerves, unlike the others, who seemed to have nerves of steel. The producer issued the cast with tiny liquorice sweets called 'imps' to help our voices. Even though the fellow I was talking to on stage was only a couple of feet from me, I had to shout at him as though he were deaf as a post. Everything we said had to be aimed at the boys in the back row. So the producer said.

During rehearsals I was told, 'There'll be a door over there' (i.e., in the wing), but it didn't in fact materialise until immediately before the actual performance. This point is important to remember. In the opening scene I had to answer the doorbell to admit the prospective private secretary who was calling for an interview, and I, not having seen the door before, didn't know whether to pull it towards me or push it from me. As luck would have it, I backed a loser, for in trying to open it I pulled the door beyond the wrong side of its frame and there it stuck, leaving an opening of only six inches. From that position I could not budge it one way or the other, and after some final pushing and pulling I gave up. The audience were laughing in a nervous sort of way, and as for me, I was dying. Turning to my companion on stage, meaning to make some cover-up remark such as, 'You ought to see about having this door repaired', wasn't I just in time to see the parson sitting astride the window frame in obvious pain, struggling in an ungainly manner to climb through. The audience was now roaring with delight, which completely unnerved us all, and from then on everything went wrong that could possibly go wrong.

The Colonel, arriving just after lunch, said it was no matter, he wasn't hungry anyway, but would love a piece of pie. A dish of bread-and-butter pudding, specially prepared by Cook, was served to him, and he was obliged to eat it sitting on his own at a small table on the stage. He nearly choked on the first mouthful for, unknown to us, some joker had sprinkled the pie liberally with salt. The culprit was never found, which when all is said and done was lucky for him.

Too bad the Colonel's lines required him to say after the first spoonful, 'By Jove, this is capital pie', and even more unfortunate that he should have to scoff the lot. Between mouthfuls he was muttering, 'I'll murder whoever done this, I'll swing for him.'

Willie Redmond, producer and prompter, blood pressure boiling in the thousands, was demanding to know what was keeping him.

Halfway through the meal the Colonel had to tell the audience, 'This is the nicest pie I've ever tasted', so I suppose in the circumstances he couldn't very well abandon it. The producer barked, 'Well then, for heaven's sake get stuck into it – do you think we can hang around all day?' When the Colonel finally finished, he got up and staggered off stage. Willie was stunned. 'Where d'you think you're going, you're not supposed – '

'Please sir, I'm goin' to be sick.'

'Sick? You can't get sick on me now! Come back here – ' but the Colonel was gone.

I thought Willie would have a fit. And wasn't I the unlucky man to be due out on stage just then? 'Get out there, you,' he said urgently. 'Go on, quick, what are you waiting for? We can't leave them gawking at a blank stage.'

'But sir, there's nobody to talk to out there, what can I do?'

'Do something, anything,' and with that he gave me an almighty push that sent me slithering sideways to the centre of the stage. In despair I looked back for inspiration, but he was no help at all. The whole school was enjoying my misfortune.

'Sing a song, do a dance, do *something* for God's sake,' the producer hissed, 'only don't just stand there like a stupid fool.'

From my small repertoire of songs I chose 'Goodbye Ol' Ship of Mine'. The hall roared, the Brothers leading the laughter, and I must say I expected better from them. My choice of song was wrong, I know, and straightaway I realised this – not because it had nothing to do with the play, but because too late I remembered that I didn't know all the words. It was hell out there on my own, I can tell you, dreading the awful moment when the words would dry up. The boys seemed to guess the position I was in, for their noise and impatience grew by the minute. Full well I knew now just how the African missionary I'd been reading about must have felt as, standing in the stewpot, he looked at the native cannibals dancing around, impatient for him to come to the boil. Luckily, my bacon was saved by the timely return of the Colonel, an ashen-faced physical wreck, so different from the dapper character who had first come on. The audience, Brothers and all, were in convulsions of laughter, under cover of which the producer demanded to know where the Colonel's moustache was.

'My moustache,' said the Colonel in alarm, whipping a hand up to his empty lip. 'Sir, I must have left it outside the door.'

'Oh my God, what the hell's it doing out there?'

'Sir, it's in the sick.'

And then we saw what the audience was laughing at. Probably by dint of the Colonel's hard retching, the buttons of his flies had come undone and the cushion underneath, inserted to add to his girth, stuck out like straw in a discarded teddy bear. He quickly wheeled around, and with his back facing the audience began to adjust himself. I was told later that from the hall he looked like someone just finishing a slash in the bushes.

Of course the play fell apart, and of course we all forgot our lines. Well, what do you expect? And as for our exits and entrances, sure they went out the window altogether. Later on, I was on the left of the stage as the audience sees it – where I was supposed to be, I might add – peering into the wings with my hand shading the light from my eyes and shouting: 'Who's that I see coming up the drive? Why, if it isn't the Colonel. *What ho there, Colonel!*'

From behind me, in the opposite wings, came an anguished whisper. 'Pssst! Joe! This way! I'm over here!' Never was undiluted despair expressed so succinctly.

I don't know how the audience heard the Colonel, but they did. One lad fell off his stool. And if that wasn't bad enough, imagine their uproar when they saw this bulge, unmistakably the Colonel, slowly make its way through the narrow space between the backdrop and the gable end of the hall, inching over to my side of the stage. I was mortified, having to stand there for ages pretending not to know what was going on. The Colonel eventually came in from the 'drive' spluttering and coughing, smothered in dust, and with all the appearance of having just returned from the Zulu Wars again. For the next five minutes everything he had to say was prefaced by an up-ward '*whew*' as he blew cobwebs from his face with his lower lip. Under cover of the noise from the hall he resumed his threats. '*Whew*, this is all his fault. Wait till I get me hands on the fella that doctored me puddin'. *Whew*, I'll spifflicate 'im, I'll massacree 'im.' It was hard to recognise in the Colonel the same fella who had played the Boy Jesus in Pearse's play *Iosagáin* only last year.

'I hope yer not lookin' at me then,' I said to him, 'for I know nothin' about your perishin' puddin'.'

The producer was in a terrible state watching his produc-tion going down the swalley-hole, powerless to retrieve it. Frantically flicking over the pages of the script, he asked, 'What are those fools going on about out there? Where are we, where does it say that?' and, not getting a reply, 'Will someone *please* tell me where we are?'

I am cursed with a literal mind, so I innocently told him we were in the recreation hall doing a play. His face turned purple. Froth appeared on his lips. The poor man was on the verge of an apoplectic fit, or whatever you call it. And listen, only I was on stage in full view of everyone I mightn't be here now telling about it!

Near the end of the play came a kind of grand finale when most of the cast were on stage, and the Colonel, turning to the parson (the private secretary), whom he was seeing for the first time, asked in surprise: 'Why, who are you, sir, and what are you doing here, may I ask?' and was to be answered by a meek and hesitant, 'Er, by this time I really don't know.' Flinging the script away, the producer said, loud enough to be heard out front, 'You're not the only one; that goes for me too.'

The curtain fell to a standing ovation. (Well, to be honest it didn't actually fall; it sluggishly unrolled to a point two-thirds of the way down, and there it stuck fast, the cast having to stoop under it to take our bows out front.) There was great excite-ment. A few Brothers came backstage, and to my amazement shook our hands, clapped us on the back and told us we were brilliant. But I knew to differ. There and then I mentally scratched 'Dramatic Actor' from the top of my list of possible careers on leaving school. It now read: 'Aviator, Arctic Explorer, Engine Driver, Conductor (band, not bus)', in that order.

In his speech of thanks from the stage Brother George said the play was easily the funniest ever produced in the history of the school. I was flabbergasted. As far as I was aware it wasn't a comedy at all but a drama full of intrigue and double-dealing. There was not a single funny line in it that I could see – not one! To be strictly honest, we hadn't ever rehearsed it from beginning to end, only in patches, if you know what I mean, so the overall picture of it – what it was all about – escaped me entirely.

And guess what! At the post mortem next day I was the one who was blamed for what the producer called the 'fiasco'. It was the first time I heard the word, so it stuck in my mind. Everything fell apart after I banjaxed the door in the first act, he claimed. 'You're a Jonah on the stage. As an actor you're a walking disaster area. Don't go within a mile of a stage ever again.'

Says I to meself, 'Begob an' there's no fear of that. I'm cured.' And I meant it.

And yet, you're not going to believe this, but about five years after I left school, when I was an orchestra member (mark you) of the Drimnagh Amateur Musical and Dramatic Society (I played the oboe, in case you don't know), wasn't I dragooned into the part of a Roman soldier in an Easter Passion play to be staged in the newly built School Hall. The part had been rehearsed by a young butcher's apprentice who was now in hospital after chopping off a finger the day before. Wasn't that a bit of bad luck – for me, I mean? For wasn't I press-ganged into the role at short notice, seeing as how the orchestra wasn't needed in any case.

How the guy came to be cast for that part I don't know, because he was only the size of a pint. (Well, I do know. His sister was doing a line with the producer.) His costume was miles too small for me, and as my bad luck would have it, wasn't it Sunday, and the theatrical costumiers, Gings of Dame Street, were shut.

It took me an hour to get squeezed into the Roman soldier's costume, consisting in the main of a skirt and a fake leather affair for a breastplate. As for the skirt, I had seen longer skirts on kilted boys of the Comerford School of Dancing doing a hornpipe. Let me put it this way: whoever claims she invented the miniskirt decades later can forget it. It was me. Not alone that, but all the soldiers had long staves, except in my case the staff I got was far too short. In the dressing room I asked Joseph of Arimathea what I was expected to do with it, and I won't tell you what he said, but I decided to use it as a walking stick instead.

On stage, as I was walking around a group of Roman soldiers sitting on their hunkers by a mock camp fire it dawned on me with a shock that the front six rows of the audience must be having a panoramic view of what was under my skirt. This was enough to knock my lines baw-ways in my brain. I was telling the squatting group that with my own two ears I had heard the Accused say he would destroy the Temple and re-build it in three days, when everyone knew it had taken Herod the Great forty-six years to build. Only I called him Henry the Eighth. The audience woke up laughing, and continued to laugh at my efforts to recover: 'Er . . . I don't mean him o' course; he isn't alive yet. I mean Herod the Eighth. No, I don't mean him either . . . '

'What you mean to say is,' cut in one of the others (who wasn't supposed to talk anyway), 'what you mean to say is "Henry the Great . . . " er, no – I don't mean . . . now you have me at it . . . '

That was the moment the Passion play went down the tubes and reappeared again as a comedy of errors.

I forgot to tell you that I had a double role to play, a character called Nick O'Demus. I had six or seven minutes to change costumes, and it was soon apparent that it couldn't possibly be done in that time. An unscheduled interval had to be announced,

*Scene from the operetta Wallace performed by the boys
of Carriglea Park School in 1927
(Photo courtesy of Dún Laoghaire Institute of
Art, Design and Technology)*

which Father Traynor, the diminutive parish priest, availed of
to admonish the audience from the curtain-front. He reminded
them in no uncertain terms that it was a sacred play and that
anyone who laughed from now on would be thrown out of the
hall, even if he had to do it himself. That would have been
worth seeing.

My body must have swollen from the heat of the stage
lights, because four apostles couldn't get me out of the soldier's
outfit. They had to cut it off me in the end, opening up the seams.
The producer, St Peter and prompter (all in one), fumed through
his false beard on seeing the costume lying in shreds – as he
thought – on the floor. The Virgin Mary told him to keep his
shirt on, and wouldn't she sew it back together again as new by

an' by, and Gings wouldn't be any the wiser. When St Peter was excited, everything gushed out at once. He said, 'That'll need a bloody miracle and who asked you to stick your shovel in anyway, and I'm worse, for what the bloody hell was I thinking of when I gave the part to yer man, wasn't everything going grand like clockwork until that eejit came on. The guy's a walking disaster, that's what he is.'

I was thinking, 'Where have I heard that before?'

Isn't it funny how one actor's simple mistake – a slip of the tongue, you might say – can have a domino effect right through to the end of a play, affecting everybody else as it goes along? Take, for instance, the final scene – 'The Resurrection' – and, mark you, I wasn't even on stage. Remember that.

There was a large wooden wheel standing on its edge. This was the 'stone' in front of the sepulchre. It was probably a vat lid borrowed by someone working in Guinness' brewery. Anyway, the idea was that the lights would go out, the 'stone' would be rolled aside, and after half a minute or so the lights would come back on, plus a spotlight pre-set to shine directly into the sepulchre to show that it was empty. Well, right on cue the lights went out. It was a solemn moment – awe-inspiring, even. You could feel the hairs rising on your mane; even the audience were moved, for to give them their due you could hear the proverbial pin drop. Suddenly, in the pitch dark, the atmosphere was shattered by: 'Oof! Jaysis, will yez get the bloody thing off me fut!'

I'll pass over the shambles that followed, and the dreadful pall of embarrassment and shame that hung over us after it was all over. As I said, I wasn't even on stage for that final scene, but I'll give you three guesses as to who was blamed. Right first go. Me! There was murder at the post-mortem the following day and I was ballyragged left, right and centre. There was talk of a letter of apology having to be sent to the priests and nuns, but Pontius Pilate (who else?) came out strongly in favour of doing nothing at all. (I wasn't long enough in the Society at the time to know the members except by their name in the play.)

And I'd love to be able to say that he said he'd wash his hands of the whole business if any letter was sent, but I mustn't exaggerate. He did want to know what all the fuss was about, and said he saw no need for an apology. In short, he demanded to know if you couldn't say 'Jaysis' in a passion play, when could you say it? There was no answer to that, so the matter was dropped. But even though everyone agreed that I was innocent of the remark which caused all the stir, the general consensus was that the whole play was a complete flop because of my initial mistake. Can you beat that?

'From now on,' they told me, 'don't ever go near the stage; just stick to yer oboe.' And I didn't and I did, in that order.

22

BROTHER TREACY'S CLASS

Let's go back to my schooldays. In the spring of 1937, I think, we heard a rumour that the school band was to be broken up. It burst on us like a bombshell. It had hardly time to circulate before we realised that it was a fact. We saw our instruments, music parts and stands – the lot – disappear before our eyes. In the space of one hour, everything having the remotest connection with the band, including the box the conductor stood on when conducting, was loaded onto a lorry and driven away. It was as though the band had sunk without trace. Naturally we, the band members, were upset because of the haste surrounding the whole business – and the secrecy too. We were more annoyed by the latter. One lad remarked how it was a wonder they didn't wait until after dark, which I thought very clever of him. The band – the school's pride and joy – had been a most valuable asset all round, especially to us musicians; it was the biggest thing in our lives. We tried figuring the reason for ourselves. Maybe the school couldn't afford to keep it going (though as for that, it seemed to us to be self-supporting, from its engagement fees), or maybe the school itself needed funding, and selling the band was a way of raising the money. We never did solve the mystery.

Willie Redmond, the bandmaster, stayed on and worked alongside Mr Dillon, the tailor, in the tailors' shop, but maybe his heart wasn't in it, because he quit soon after. He was practically one of ourselves because he was a past pupil, and we were sorry to see him go. He joined a Capuchin Novitiate in County Galway, adopting the name Brother Dennis, and we kept in touch by letter. He wasn't too happy there, because he quit when it came to the point of taking his vows. He emigrated to England then, and we lost touch. Nearly fifty years later I met Gerry Devereux in Dublin. Gerry had played tenor trombone in the band, and was now proprietor of one of only five hand-tailoring businesses still surviving in Ireland. From him I learned that Willie Redmond – or Liam, as he now preferred to be known – was alive and well in England after all these years. Thanks to that chance encounter with Gerry, I got back in touch with Liam. He lived in retirement in a small cottage in Hertfordshire.

He lent me some interesting memoirs of his later career, from which I learned that he had devoted his life to teaching tailoring and cutting to handicapped people in various institutions there. It was an impressive dossier, and I thought that he deserved a special honour for his lifetime of charitable work. I smiled to see several playbills and cuttings relating to shows and revues which he had staged for charity down the years in the institutions where he worked.

As a boy, Liam had been one among many in our school who had no parents or relatives to visit them. They never got presents at Christmas or birthdays, nor did they have any Christmas or August breaks, because they had no homes. Liam never married in later life, and so never acquired relatives or loved ones, though I am sure he would not have been short of friends among the poor and disadvantaged. Liam and I wrote to each other regularly, until his death at the age of eighty-eight in 1995.

During my final week in the Master's class we were told that an examination in maths was being held to select the top six boys for inclusion in Brother Treacy's class, to be tutored specially for the Post Office entrance examination. That was a fateful day. The cards on which six mathematical problems were printed were so distributed that no boy received a card similar to that of the boy on either side (in case there should be cribbing). Maths wasn't my strong subject so I was taut with nerves, because the results would be crucial to my future, which would be either in the Post Office or in a trade.

Imagine my surprise and delight when I was told a few days later that I was one of the successful six. My many friends in the trades tried to persuade me to join them in the workshop, and argued convincingly that a boy with a skill in tailoring or shoemaking would earn lots more money and would always have a job – in fact, he could pick and choose among jobs. The Brother saw my dilemma and said, 'It's up to you, but you have only until tomorrow to decide. I'll want your answer first thing in the morning.'

I couldn't go to sleep for ages that night. Until then, everything was decided for me and here I had to determine something I knew would affect my life forever. It was a frightening thought. The next morning I told Brother George that I would go to Brother Treacy's classes. 'I never doubted you,' he said.

Brother Treacy was over seventy, and had come back from retirement the year before to tutor an elite class as an experiment. He had 100 per cent success, for all his class passed the Post Office examination. I knew him only from having seen him at Mass and evening devotions, but he had a great reputation as a teacher. He was slight of build and feeble, silver-haired and stooped with age; the skin on his face and hands, pale and stretched (almost translucent), was like a film of warm candle-grease over a filigree of fine red and purple veins. He gave the impression of being always cold, even in summertime, and was rarely seen without his jacket, over a shabby, shiny, ankle-length soutane. He was to leave a lasting impression and influence upon me, as nobody else has done. By his special methods and endearing manner he transformed our attitude towards school. In place of hatred born of fear there was soon a great love for learning, so that we thirsted for more. His methods contrasted notably with those of the Master. Force was absent: he chose to lead rather than drive. He showed gentle kindness and amazing patience and understanding, which encouraged us greatly. We were drawn closer to knowledge so eagerly that we begrudged moments spent outside his classroom. Our sole purpose was to please him.

He began with the basics, as though to say, 'Forget all you learned before', which applied even to our handwriting, for he

192

showed each pupil individually how he wished him to hold the pen. As we had become accustomed to holding it 'incorrectly', it was some little time before we adapted, but in the end all six of us acquired the same neat copperplate hand amazingly similar to his own. He didn't like fountain pens, and when I won the pen in the School Sports he asked me not to use it. 'It will ruin your handwriting, you can't possibly hold it the way I showed you,' he said, and I was disappointed. However, I did not do badly, because I swapped it with someone for a mouth organ.

The pen in use in those days consisted of a slim wooden handle with a metal section at the bottom into which a renewable brass nib was inserted. These pens, common to all schools, were but a step removed from the quill-pens of olden days. A glass inkwell sat in a hole in the front of each desk, and we had to dip the nib in the ink frequently, taking care not to take up too much ink at a time – a sure way of blotting the page.

Brother Treacy had a special way of teaching Irish too. Disregarding the Department of Education's regulations, he taught Irish entirely through English. This was of enormous help in understanding the complicated rules of grammar. He gave painstaking attention to English and Irish essays also: he arrived in class every morning with an essay written into his own copybook the previous evening. He read it aloud to give us a broad outline of what we should try to do, after which we discussed the structure and content, paragraph by paragraph. Only then were we allowed to proceed to our own essay. The closer we adhered to his structures and ideas, the more he liked it. He was a lovely, lovely man.

He came from Tipperary, or 'Tip-prary' as he pronounced it, and many a history lesson he embroidered with anecdotes of his childhood years, as for instance his memory of seeing a penny-farthing bicycle for the first time. He described the people of the town rushing to the street en masse to see this extraordinary machine lumbering down the main street, and he remembered the old man beside him exclaiming in amazement:

'Why, it went by like a . . . a . . . an elephant!' His parents used to describe to him the days when Charles Bianconi organised coach races between Clonmel and Cahir so as to popularise travelling by coach and to allay fears about its safety. A century later, in the early days of flying, transworld air races were sponsored to promote travel by air and to demonstrate how safe and reliable it was.

We found it hard to believe that Brother Treacy had lived in the same period as Charles Stewart Parnell, Gladstone, Isaac Butt and Michael Davitt, people we were reading about in our history books! In our eyes they were but vague spectres from a dim and distant past. These great men had been embroiled in the Land Question – Home Rule and the like, mammoth problems of their day. Now these very problems counted for little and were regarded by us as mere phases of history, taken for granted in the Ireland of our time. Alas, the struggles of our forefathers were only of academic interest, for city boys were we, having no interest in the land whatsoever. How different from our forebears!

The Brother talked at length and in detail about the Land War – the wholesale evictions of tenant farmers, and Gladstone's several attempts to end it by Land Acts in the 1880s. We could tell by the way he spoke that he was drawing on recollections of scenes personally witnessed, and we heard about it in more detail than was found in the history book. So graphically did he describe one of Parnell's public meetings (at which he must have been present in his youth) that something of Parnell's dynamism and charisma shone through, as if we too had been there. We could feel the excitement of that meeting, share the crowd's deeply felt grievances about unjust treatment at the hands of absentee landlords, and almost smell the heavy tobacco smoke in the packed, paraffin-lit hall. He told us of that era of our history in a sad, intimate way, and when he was finished he remained for a while gazing vacantly at the floor, disinclined to proceed to the next subject, still under the spell of the age and reluctant to let the memories pass.

Whether it was at play or work, at school or trade, at prayers in chapel or in the refectory for meals, all the school had to be in their appointed places under supervision, and it was a punishable offence for anyone to be elsewhere without special permission. Not so Brother Treacy's class. We stayed apart from the rest after classroom hours to study our 'tasks' or homework, and were unsupervised. We even studied in bed, though we had to battle with distractions from the gramophone – Sir Harry Lauder, Gerard Crofts, Peter Dawson, and John McCormack, who were our pop stars in those days. I had a private arrangement with the nightwatchman to be wakened at half past five every morning to revise my homework, because studying didn't come easy to me – not like the others, who could sleep their heads off for another hour and yet know all the answers.

Paddy O'Dea was one of those. He managed to come late to class every morning. So persistent was he that he must have been late on purpose, just to make us laugh. Lee, sitting on my right, also had a reckless sense of fun. While looking the Brother straight in the face, he could throw his voice without moving his lips. I was blamed for talking – never Lee. Once he gave a hilarious commentary on a 'hairy molly' caterpillar's attempt at climbing up the outside of the windowpane. He highlighted every pause, every twist of the insect's head and body, every falter and stumble; he did it as if it were the caterpillar speaking. And as it finished the exhausting climb to the top, it said, 'Well would ya believe it, there's nothin' up here after all me trouble.' The coincidence of its falling off just at that moment was too much for me, and I laughed uncontrollably. I was ordered to stand outside the door. The danger now was that the Superior might happen along and see me, and then I would be in real trouble. Many years later I heard this story. A boy was supposed to have been punished so severely for a similar offence the year before that he hadn't been allowed remove his shirt in the washroom for a fortnight to avoid exposing the marks of his punishment.

I don't believe that story. Firstly, a beating so severe had never to my knowledge been given in the school. It could not have escaped my knowledge; it would have been the talk of the school for days. Secondly, such a punishment would have been out of proportion to the offence – a more likely one would have been expulsion from Brother Treacy's elite class, and that, I know for a fact, had not happened the boy in question, since he had passed the Post Office examination the year before.

Yet my informant insisted that severe floggings were given in the school in our time, and cited the punishment of boys who, he said, had been caught in acts of mutual masturbation. That such floggings could have taken place – for whatever reason – without my knowledge in that small world in which we lived was simply not possible. I remain unconvinced. Further, I'm certain that the story is not true for the reason that it was entirely out of character for the Brother allegedly involved.

I was hardly outside the classroom door when I heard footsteps approaching, and not wishing to get into the Superior's bad books, I looked for somewhere to hide. There was a large laundry skip under the stairs, directly opposite the classroom, and into it I climbed and closed the wicker lid down over me just in time. To my dismay, the footsteps stopped. Had I been heard? Would the lid be raised, or would the classroom door be opened? I held my breath, and it was lucky that I did, otherwise my breathing would have made the wickerwork creak and I would surely have been discovered. Thanks to the development of my lungs from having played the oboe in the band, to hold my breath for what seemed like ten minutes was to me a mere trifle. To my intense relief, Brother George went into the classroom and I breathed out again. He sometimes called in to talk with Brother Treacy, and as far as I was concerned he could stay as long as he liked this time, for I was prepared to crouch in the basket no matter how long it took. Then more footsteps came. This time they stopped. I was wheeled out to the yard, and realised to my horror that I was on my way to the Mary Magdalen Laundry in Dún Laoghaire! 'No you're not,' says I to myself, and before the laundrymen could lift basket, laundry, me and all into the van and drive away, I leapt out, to their cries of amazement, composed my hair and clothes, and legged it back.

I entered the classroom. The distance between the door and my desk seemed like half a mile, but I walked it as nonchalantly as if I had only been returning from 'the yard'. Brother Treacy was still engaged in conversation with Brother George. I banked on his silence, on his reluctance to get me into serious trouble, and he didn't let me down. Presently we learned the reason for the Superior's visit: the date for the exam had been announced.

The exam for Post Office boy-messengers took place in December 1937. That was before free secondary education, so there was a large number of candidates. Consequently, there were two exam centres in Dublin and one in each provincial city. My centre was in Ely Place in Dublin.

The exam was from nine until five-thirty, with a break for lunch at one o'clock. I hadn't brought a lunch and had no money, apart from my return bus fare so, accompanied by Ferdinand McCrossan (a fellow candidate whose acquaintance I had just made that day, and who was destined to be a lifelong friend), I went to the National Gallery nearby. Admission was free, and it was raining. I had never been in such a place before and was amazed. The only pictures I had ever seen were the holy pictures in the convent. Imagine my surprise on coming across a nude. I gestured urgently to Ferdie, saying, 'C'mere and look at this one; it's not even finished.'

'Yes it is,' Ferdie said in a superior tone. 'It's supposed to be a woman, and they haven't got one,' which I thought was hilarious. We were promptly ordered outside by the uniformed man in charge.

In the months that followed the exam, while we waited for the results, our routines in school didn't change. We continued our studies without let-up, because if we had succeeded we would sit an oral Irish exam, and if we had failed, we were within the age limits to sit the written exam again. Both possibilities were covered.

23

GOODBYE CARRIGLEA

As the boys filed out of the chapel in twos after seven o'clock Mass on a cold morning in the spring of 1938, I noticed the Master scanning the faces of the slowly moving column and thought, 'Someone's in trouble already today.' My heart stopped when he stretched his hand towards me, but smiling in unaccustomed friendliness, he drew me aside to show me the examination results in the *Irish Independent*. 'Here, read it for yourself,' he gushed excitedly. 'Every boy passed, but you were best of all.' I had taken second place, and the rest of the class took the places from third to seventh on the list. Calling out the other boys, he shook hands, and a stranger watching would have thought we were the best of friends.

It was standard practice in those days for the results of government exams to be published in the newspapers, and of course we got written notification (in Irish) as well, together with the date for the oral Irish exam. That the school should have scooped six of the first seven places in Ireland was a wonderful tribute to Brother Treacy, and great was the hullabaloo in the refectory that morning. He seemed to be little affected by the results, however, for it was 'business as usual', and we did not even get a half-day as reward. In fact, we worked even harder, preparing for the oral Irish exam in a month's time. Even though this was my first oral Irish exam – one of many that I was to sit down the years – I don't have any recollection of it, except that we all passed.

The next phase was the medical examination, for which I saw Doctor Frost at his surgery in Dún Laoghaire. He examined my eyes, ears, teeth, heart and lungs, and measured my height and weight, entering his findings in a pile of forms on his desk. I refused to comply when he asked me to drop my trousers, however, getting very agitated, but I gave in eventually after a great deal of persuasion and threats of cancelling the whole business altogether. Then he asked me to pass water into an oval bowl and I, not understanding, spat into it. 'No, no,' he said, 'pass water – you know, go to the toilet.' When he saw that I now understood, he went behind a screen.

As I filled the bowl I was thinking what a clever doctor he must be to know that I badly wanted to go, just by feeling me down there and telling me to cough.

Then I emptied the contents down the washbasin.

The doctor rushed out with a cry. 'What *are* you doing? I want that for analysis,' and whipping from my hand the bowl in which just about a thimbleful remained, he added with annoyance, 'This will probably do, but if it doesn't, you'll have to come back.' It must have been ample, because I didn't have to see him again.

After a few weeks we were notified to attend for duty in the GPO in Dublin at 9 AM on 23 March 1938, which happened to be two days before my fifteenth birthday.

On the day before, which was my last day in the school, I was sent to the tailors' shop to collect my new suit, shirt, tie, shoes and socks, and told to put them on in the dormitory. I took the stairs two at a time, although strange to say my feelings were mixed, now that the day of my leaving had come. On the one hand, this had been my happy home for years, shared with many friends, most of whom I would never see again. On the other, it was a major turning point in my life – special, magical in fact. There I was, putting on long trousers for the first time (long trousers were worn only by grown men in those days). In the short space of time it took to change my clothes I left my childhood behind me forever.

But what a disappointment on looking in the mirror! The trousers were terrible – so tight and narrow that they gave me a spindle-shanked, gawky, pipe-cleaner look. 'How on earth am I going to find the nerve to walk abroad in them?' I thought, for well I knew the terrible jeering I'd get when the boys saw me. The trousers couldn't have been more uncomfortable. Made of coarse, hairy, woollen material, they clung closely to me, and itched in the most embarrassing places. And to think how eagerly I had looked forward to my first 'longers'! Is it any wonder they were known as drainpipes? It didn't occur to me to go back to the tailors' shop for a better fitting. When Brother George saw me, I expected some criticism, but he passed no remark and I didn't want to complain.

The shoes were a better proposition, and what a relief after wearing heavy, hobnailed boots – it used be said that one needed only to lift them, they'd fall themselves. I couldn't avoid the boys on my way to report to the Brother, and so self-conscious was I of my appearance, so embarrassed by their playful but hurtful banter and criticism, that I had only one desire, and that was to be gone from the scene without delay. Small wonder that I forgot to say goodbye to the Matron and the Brothers – even Brother Treacy himself, to whom I owed so much. Only that I was ordered to report to Brother George when ready, I might have fled at once. But I had one last act to perform before leaving: namely, to exchange with Paddy Carr his pocket watch for my half a crown (twelve and a half pence) – the sum total of fifteen months' hard saving.

Brother George saw me to the bus stop at Dean's Grange Cross, and I expected him to return to the school when the bus came, but he boarded with me. If we talked on the way I don't remember it, but on arriving in the city he treated me to tea and sweet cakes in Noonan's Café on O'Connell Street, near the bridge. 'Looking ahead twenty years,' he said, 'I see you driving your own car, and dining in places like this. But I hope you won't be slopping your tea into your saucer like that,' he added with a smile, forgetting that cups and saucers were unknown in school – for that matter, so were spoons – tea being served in enamel mugs, already milked and sugared. We chatted for ages, he doing most of the talking, as though reluctant to bring the meal to an end. We were equals now I felt, two adults. If I kept in touch with my books, he told me, I could improve myself in my career because there was great scope for self-advancement in the Post Office. Strong as the pull towards mother and home was after ten long years of absence (and how many times had I longed to be reunited with her?), the desire to go back with the Brother to school was stronger at that moment. Had he asked me to return with him and sit a higher exam the following year, I'd have jumped at the offer. Why not? I was leaving a year ahead of time, sixteen being the normal leaving age in the school; I hadn't expected to be leaving a year early. However, the offer wasn't made. Our meal, long extended by conversation, ended at last and we said goodbye outside. I dallied after he left, and must have looked a curious sight, waving to his receding figure with one hand and wiping my tears with the other.

A week later a parcel of well-pawed school books came by post – Irish and English grammars, history and geography books, smudged and underlined, pages patched with Scotch tape and pencilled notes in the margins. A note enclosed said: 'Remember my advice. These will help you.'

The day after I left school, I enlisted in the lowest grade of the Irish Civil Service, namely, Post Office boy-messenger, or 'telegram boy'. About a dozen other boys, including my five schoolmates, started at the same time, our seniority permanently determined by our place in the exam. As the Inspector of Messengers, Mr Charlie Garrett, collected our completed initiation forms on the top floor of the GPO, he quipped: 'Welcome to the Post Office, lads; you now have a job for life and a pension after.'

Later on we went to John Ireland and Company on Ellis Quay for our uniforms, and I was wearing boots again. The tunic had a single row of brass buttons down the front, which from now on I would have to polish with Brasso every day, for it was an offence to have dull buttons. The tunic's high, throat-hugging neckband (which fastened tightly under the chin) forced you to keep your head erect, and was to prove extremely uncomfortable in summer. Even so, should a boy be seen by an outdoor Inspector with an unfastened tunic, he was charged with a 'serious offence'. A small oval badge, pinned to the breast of my tunic, conveyed my identity to all as T51, and I was officially addressed only by that number while serving in the telegram delivery room.

For a boy with my background, to work as a telegram boy in 1930s Dublin was a traumatic experience. My hitherto sheltered life left me utterly unprepared for the world into which I was catapulted. Furthermore, I was an absolute misfit among about fifty boys, whose background could not have been more different from mine. To say that I was tossed into a deep sea, at the mercy of a shoal of killer sharks might be putting it a bit strongly but there were times when I felt that that was what had happened to me. For months I went to work trembling from fear, and indeed it was only by sheer guts and will-power that I managed to get there some days.

Amongst the boys there was a hard core of 'hard chaws', rough and tough, whose code seemed to be 'dislike of the unlike', and I appeared to be their natural target. In time I realised that I must conform to the general behaviour, but I was slow to learn, and had a rough time for long enough.

What set me apart in their eyes – even from my ex-schoolmates – I don't know. I was disoriented and slow to make friends, and thus may have given the impression that I considered myself a cut above the rest. They had a special dislike for Carriglea boys anyway, but I felt that there was extra disdain in my case. Letting the air out of my bike, name-calling and jeering and hiding my cap so as to have me put on report for being improperly dressed were the usual torments, but there was worse than that. Opening my trousers and smearing me with the cleaning paste used by the mechanics to clean their oily hands (a mix of paste and coarse sand) caused me deep embarrassment and distress. My situation wasn't helped by the fact that I didn't understand them; expressions strange to my ears flew about in all directions, and what are now referred to as four-letter words appeared in all their conversations with amazing frequency. Some boys, with great bravado, went out of their way to shock their listeners, but even their best efforts were wasted on me. The locker-room jokes passed over my head, and I was jeered and called a 'Holy Joe' for not laughing. Soon I learned that by reacting as raucously as the loudest of them, I made things easier for myself. I am sure young people today will find hard to believe how a fifteen-year-old lad could have been as artless and guileless as I. The fact is, I was like a space alien in a new world, a stranger to its language, customs and behaviour.

Of course there were exceptions among the boys, and for protection I sought their company whenever opportunity allowed, but they, alas, were not always able to protect me from the roughnecks. Some were in my batch of newcomers – rookies – and got their share of 'stick' themselves. My experiences caused me great unhappiness, distress and depression at a time when I was struggling to adapt to a completely new life.

I was on foot-duty for the first few weeks, and did the short trips to nearby offices of the *Irish Independent*, *Irish Press* and *Irish Times*, and to two coal merchants, Donnelly's and Doherty's, all of whom got telegrams in an almost unbroken chain throughout the day. City-centre hotels also received telegrams from messengers on foot. On Wellington Quay, near the Clarence Hotel, stood the premises of one of Dublin's prestigious opticians. A banner across the top of its window proclaimed them to be opticians to the pope, while in Temple Bar, directly behind, stood a small shoe-repair shop whose window bore the legend COBBLERS TO THE KING.

In those days, important businesses in the city centre – banks, insurance companies and the like – employed a uniformed adult messenger or porter in their public office. The most flamboyantly dressed were the bank messengers, in silk top hat, butterfly collar, swallowtail coat, striped trousers and bright (saffron or scarlet) waistcoat, with gold watch-chain. These men, elite among company messengers, were a familiar sight, walking leisurely, with great dignity, and never in a hurry, carrying documents in a briefcase between their branch offices.

I had to know how to ride a bicycle – it was one of the conditions of my employment – but as I had never had access to a bicycle when at school, I had no way of learning. I told a white lie when filling in my induction form, thinking I'd bluff my way out of the problem when it arose. I didn't know there would be a cycling test, so it was a shock when I was ordered outside by the Inspector and given a bicycle. In disbelief I heard him say, 'Let me see you ride to the end of the street, turn round and come back again. Off you go.'

The bike was a high, heavy, cumbersome James model, beside which I could hardly walk. My first problem was how to save it from falling and pulling me after it; the second, how to mount it. I was shaking from nerves. For once, my good luck was in, for there came on the scene at the crucial moment a friend of the Inspector's (of the 'long lost' variety, it seemed) who engaged him in conversation and completely absorbed his attention while I wobbled precariously up the side of the GPO building. I dismounted at the end of the street by letting myself fall off, and on observing the two men at the far end still engrossed, I wheeled the bike to the opposite side and, hidden by the Capitol Theatre, which projected into the street, remounted and wobbled back again. So as not to be seen falling off, I cycled past the pair unnoticed, and fell off behind them. Obviously the Inspector had forgotten about me, for he said with some surprise when I interrupted him, 'What is it, T51? Oh yes, there you are! Still in one piece then? OK, you can report inside for cycle duty.'

It took only a day's work (eight hours) for me to become a proficient cyclist in the thick of Dublin's traffic. If it wasn't as heavy as today's traffic, it was far more chaotic. People crossed the street where they liked, for zebra crossings belonged to the future, as did traffic lights, except for a set experimentally erected at the junction of Merrion and Clare Streets. A point-duty policeman at major junctions controlled traffic in all weathers by waving his white-sleeved arms.

Tramlines were the scourge of even experienced cyclists,

and one also had to contend with a fair amount of horse-drawn traffic as well, which demanded right of way over all else. There was a twofold risk of a fall from the bike: the possibility of catching the front wheel in the tramlines, or skidding in the horse droppings which littered the streets.

Many businesses seemed reluctant to change to motorised from horse-drawn transport, among them the laundries: White Swan, White Heather, Swastika and Magdalen. Domestic washing machines were unknown, so laundries collected your linen on Monday and delivered it to your door on Saturday, laundered, ironed and cellophane-wrapped, for a small fee. Dublin's main bakeries – Boland's, Kennedy's, Downes' and Johnston, Mooney & O'Brien's – delivered bread not only to the shops but also to private houses, and used horse-drawn vans for the purpose. Scores of independent milkmen and the larger milk companies – Hughes Brothers', Tel el Kebir and Lucan Dairies – used horse-drawn floats, as did private coal-delivery men known as bellmen, because of the bell that hung from the horse's neck. The Post Office played safe by having horse-drawn and motor transport.

All streets, even the main ones, were paved with cobblestones or wooden sets; city cycling was a bone-shaking experience either way. Cobblestones and sets were equally hazardous in wet weather, when risks of skidding were high. The North Circular Road was particularly perilous midweek, when cattle were driven on the hoof from the cattle market at Hanlon's Corner all the way through the busy city to the docks at North Wall for shipment abroad. They left an almost continuous trail of cow dung on the road behind them, which was scattered in all directions by the following traffic. Senior messenger boys delivered telegrams to the suburbs on Post Office motorbikes, and serious accidents involving them were not uncommon, some resulting in broken limbs.

The Post Office took an interest in the boys' leisure activities. Once a week we had an hour's free use of the swimming pool (known as the baths) in Iveagh House, Bride Road. In addition, a large room on the top floor of the GPO was set aside as a leisure centre known as 'the Institute', where we could go after work to exercise on parallel bars, or to play table tennis and push ha'penny. Boxing gloves were also available, as I would learn to my cost.

About this time there was a popular comedian named Harry Bailey in the Queen's Theatre. He liked to use catchphrases like 'That shook yeh' and 'Are y'up, McGucken?' These became common everyday expressions. As I passed an older messenger outside the office one day, I gave him a friendly salute with 'Are y'up McGucken?', meaning, 'How are ye?' It was a way of ingratiating myself. How unfortunate for me that the boy's name was McGucken; not surprisingly, this particular catchphrase was to him as a red rag is to a bull. He flew into a rage, gripped me by the throat, and was about to bring his other fist crashing down on my face when Mr Garrett the Inspector came on the scene.

'Now, now, this is no way for you to behave,' he said. 'The Post Office in its wisdom has provided the very place where you can settle your argument in a sporting way, like gentlemen. I want to see both of you in the Institute this evening at nine, with the boxing gloves on.'

Word of the 'boxing match' soon spread among the boys and I overheard some of them arranging to come back after work to see it. There was no escape, no way out. I'd simply have to turn up – or be branded a coward forever.

A cheer from the crowd of waiting boys greeted my arrival that evening, and some were even shouting from the gallery which ran along one side of the room. My opponent, there ahead of me, had donned the lighter boxing gloves, which gave him a great advantage. My jacket and shirt were removed in a flash by dozens of helping hands, and gloves that must surely once have belonged to Primo Camera the boxing giant were jammed onto my hands and secured by yards and yards of tape. Suddenly everyone was a boxing expert.

'Plenty of footwork, Joe. Keep movin' – like this.'

'Keep them fists up all the time – are ye lookin'? – right in front of yer face, and elbows tucked in so he won't be able to touch yeh.'

There was no referee, and needless to say no Inspector. I knew I was facing slaughter, and I could do nothing about it. I began to sweat, and not from the heat. Table-tennis and other equipment was pushed to one side and the fight was on. I really tried to keep my gloves up, but it was like trying to hold a con-crete block at face level. The sheer weight of the gloves repeat-edly forced my arms to my sides, and each time a lightning left came in from McGucken, sending me crashing to the floor. One second I was upright, the next I was on my back looking up dazedly into a circle of faces, all shouting helpful hints. The dominant message was: 'Keep up yer gloves, are ye deaf or wha'?'

My opponent had a royal time using me as a punchbag. Not once had I to rise to my feet under my own steam. I was hoisted upright with monotonous regularity by dozens of seconds, and was powerless to resist.

'Jus' land one punch, Joe, an' he'll run, I know this guy. Are ye listenin'?' If it hadn't been so almighty serious, what with me being so busy getting the stuffing knocked out of me, I would have laughed. Why, the very notion of landing even one punch was completely out of the question; just keeping my gloves up was a full-time job in itself. I even tried crouching under them, but it was no use.

At last, driven to the wall by a merciless onslaught, I flop-ped to a sitting position just as my opponent's fist came for the *coup de grâce*, which landed with crashing force on the wall at the exact spot where my face had been a split-second before. There was a roar of pain from McGucken, now bent double, hugging one hand under his oxter. The fight stopped auto-matically, and why wouldn't it, since he alone had been doing the fighting? He was writhing around in agony from what turned out to be a broken wrist – only the damage wasn't known just then. I had lost the fight, but I wasn't beaten. In the dressing room I threw my opponent a haughty paraphrase of Patrick Sarsfield's taunt to the English after the Battle of the Boyne (the one about swapping kings): 'Change gloves and I'll fight you again.' At least, that's what I said, but what emerged was a meaningless splutter, owing to the fact that my lips were swollen like a couple of sausages. Wherever I went for days afterwards people thought I was trying to whistle, and while my lips did return to normal eventually, I can't say the same for my poor nose, which was never the same again.

Not until the following day did I discover that I was being hailed the winner of the fight, although one wag, who must have seen it, dubbed me 'Horizontal Boxing Champion of Ireland'. The logic was simple enough: McGucken would be out sick for weeks and I was credited with putting him there. There was a pleasant aftermath for me: from that day on I was everyone's friend, most of all to my erstwhile tormentors. I was now admitted to the herd.

24

CONCLUSION

Love was the main theme of most popular songs of the 1930s, and naturally songs like 'Mexicali Rose, I Love You', and 'Red Sails in the Sunset' hadn't been heard in school, nor one that went:

> Last night the moon was mellow
> Rosita met grand Manuelo.
> He held her like this, this lovely miss,
> Then stole a kiss, this fellow.

They had tuneful melodies that one couldn't help whistling when cycling around Dublin. Such songs were sung lustily on the boy-messengers' annual outing to Wicklow or Drogheda in summer, and at our Christmas party, the 'bun rush' in the Broadway Café, Lower O'Connell Street. I sang them gustily with the other boys, a little guiltily at first, I have to admit, wondering what the Brother Superior would have thought.

For the 'bun rush' we turned up in civilian clothes, hair drenched with hair oil and flattened smooth as though painted on our heads. Dressed like adults in miniature, three-piece suits and soft felt hats, we were like so many Bugsy Malones. Edward G. Robinson, the film star 'gangster', must have looked similar to us when in his teens. A few boys proudly brought a young girl on their arm and behaved like young gentlemen to impress her. A special area raised above the rest was reserved for them, from where they looked down their noses towards the noisy end of the room, as though the conduct here was alien to them. Tea and fancy cakes were shuttled in by waitresses until we were fit to burst. Heaven must be like this, I thought.

This experience was new and tremendously exciting. I was

fifteen, artless, bewildered, in a world I was getting to know slowly. Slowly? It would be two years before I was wise to Santa Claus (I was hanging up my stocking at seventeen) and I would be in my early twenties when I learned what were called the 'facts of life'. I might not have been alone in my ignorance, because times were far different. Today I'd be classed as a very slow learner. Let me again stress that there is a great difference between the Ireland of today and Ireland in the 1930, 1940s and 1950s. The Catholic Church was a mighty power in the land, and the people were extremely prudish, insular and inward-looking. Books and even songs were banned, many merely for being 'suggestive'. Nor did the censor always ban them directly, but was often nudged into action, and criticised in the press for being too liberal. Horizons were narrower owing in part to that strict censorship which kept from our shelves many books and magazines from abroad, chiefly from Great Britain. Some films never reached our screens, and in many of those which did, gaps were seen, left by the busy scissors of Mr James Montgomery, the Irish Film Censor. This, despite the fact that they had already passed the rigid rules of the Hays Office, the guardian of morals in America, where most of the films we saw were made, and whose regulations were regarded by Americans as strict even for them. Indeed, the cinema was considered a bad influence, and the clergy themselves were discouraged from going.

The Lenten fast was strictly kept, not so much because of pressure applied by the clergy as by those referred to as 'lay clergy', self-appointed guardians of morality and religious observance – and there were many in that category. A woman risked her good name and reputation by smoking in the street, or (heavens above!) if seen leaving a public house. That was Ireland then, the world I had burst upon from my blinkered life in an institution.

Those locker-room jokes already referred to, and considered daring and 'blue' in their day, would not even raise an eyebrow today, never mind a laugh, but would have shocked the adult dispatchers in the adjoining room had they heard them. A key word like 'knickers' in the punchline was enough to send the boys into hysterical laughter, yet many a telegram boy (myself included) died a thousand deaths when delivering a telegram to certain department stores in the city, as to reach their office a section of the store had to be traversed where ladies' nighties and various articles of female underwear were for sale in colourful array. Our every step through this female sanctum was followed by eyes registering shocked disapproval.

My starting pay in the Post Office was twelve shillings and a penny a week, which I was soon able to augment with another shilling by cleaning the official pushbikes. Twenty shillings made one pound. The allowance went to pay the hire purchase on my brand-new bicycle, whose price was £6.10.0 (six pounds and ten shillings) cash, or £7.16.0 over an eternity of three years. When I remembered that it had taken me more than a year to save two shillings and sixpence for my second-hand watch, I became terrified of the debt I had incurred, and quickly returned to the bicycle shop in Aungier Street to back out of my agreement, but failed.

My living conditions in James' Street still revolted me and when coming in and going out I looked up the street and down, prepared to hide should a workmate happen to be cycling by. The shame spurred me to action. To the City Hall I went in uniform, pretending to have a telegram for Alderman Mrs Tom Clarke. Introducing myself as a friend of Nurse Scanlon from Carriglea (which was good enough to excuse my deception), I described my living conditions at home, sparing no detail, and asked if she might help get us a corporation house, as my mother had been on the housing list for a number of years. I stressed that conditions had worsened greatly when my sister and I came home from school. She was very friendly and seemed impressed, especially on hearing that teenagers of mixed sexes had to share the same room, but said that everything depended on an inspector's report. We were all present when the inspector called, and for once I was delighted to see how horrified he was. Not long after, we were assigned a new house in Drimnagh, which was then only in the early stages of development as Dublin's newest suburb. I was delighted to have played my part, although in doing so my stepfather's nose was put out of joint, as he saw it as a challenge to him as head of the family. I shall never forget my mother's joy the day we moved to our new house, and was surprised to see that what our one room had contained required two journeys in a large van to move, even though we left behind a lot of unwanted stuff.

We were now living in a housing estate growing larger by the day, whose layout, to be understood, needed to be viewed from an aeroplane. All the houses were built to the same design and painted in similar colours, so it was hard to distinguish one road from another, and so we had trouble finding our road when we went out. The problem was solved quite by accident. In the garden outside our front door I sowed a sixpenny packet of mixed flower seeds, which happened to contain four sunflowers. They soon grew over six feet high and became a landmark by which our road was identified from a distance.

Gradually I came to know new foods: corned beef, butter, tomatoes, shell cocoa, coffee, rashers, fried and scrambled eggs, black and white pudding, fish and chips. Our own turkey and ham at Christmas would come much later. I remember tasting marmalade for the first time. It happened this way: I went cycling into the country every Sunday with Ferdinand McCrossan, my pal and fellow boy-messenger. We brought sandwiches and lemonade for the journey, and naturally we exchanged food. We sat one day on the side of the road a mile beyond Balbriggan on our way to see the round tower and ancient Celtic cross at Monasterboice in County Louth. Ferdie offered me a sandwich.

'What sort of jam is this?' I asked.

'It's not jam, it's marmalade,' Ferdie answered.

'Marm-a-lade,' I repeated slowly, parting the bread to have a look. To myself I said, 'Even the name is nice.'

'How come you never tasted marmalade before?' he asked in surprise. I made up an excuse, for to explain truthfully I should have had to reveal my shameful past and risk losing his friendship. This was it! Fear of losing valued friendships forced me to cloak my past in guilty secrecy throughout my life. By then I knew that Carriglea and all other industrial schools were notorious places in the eyes of the public at large. Every time a boy was committed to such an institution for truancy or other misdemeanours, the committal was reported in the newspapers, and although the boys were not identified by name, the schools to which they were sent received prominent mention. This practice had given my school a bad reputation, resulting in all its ex-pupils being tarred with the same brush. I was one of thousands of victims of Irish society's cruel attitude towards boys and girls with an industrial-school background, and I came to know the anguish and shame of being stigmatised and shunned. In the eyes of the public, we fell into one of two categories: we were bastards or jailbirds. Either way, we were not fit to be in society, and mothers warned their children not to have anything to do with us. The prejudice forced us to make a dark secret of our past, and most kept it from their spouses and families, taking it finally to the grave. I didn't deserve the dreadful stigma – none of us did – so no wonder I kept my past a secret from Ferdie and from my friends and colleagues down the years.

In time, Ferdie's official duties and mine sent us in different directions and we met only rarely. In 1950 I transferred to the Telephone Branch, while Ferdie remained on the postal side, sorting mails on the train between Dublin and Galway. He later became Inspector of Messengers, Charlie Garrett's job, though not Charlie's immediate successor. He retired at sixty, and sad to say only a month or two afterwards I sat weeping by his bedside in Sir Patrick Dun's Hospital, a few hours before he died of cancer.

With the exception of Joe White (who joined the RAF), my other classmates in the Post Office quit to join the Irish army at the outbreak of the Emergency, as the Second World War was known in Ireland, but whether it was to escape the fallout of our past I cannot say, for I didn't see them again. I was transferred out of the mainstream of telegram boys to indoor work in the PO Engineering Branch, where I remained until I was eighteen, at which age I became a postman.

I said that the school's public notoriety surprised me, because when I was there I saw Carriglea as it really was, and felt somehow privileged to be there. Once I had cast off the loneliness and homesickness that had plagued me in my more tender years, I knew real happiness there.

Carriglea Park Industrial School is long gone; its buildings are home to services of a different kind – it is now the Institute of Art, Design and Technology. It closed its doors to homeless boys sometime in the 1950s, and I doubt whether anyone today has heard of it who was not personally connected with it. Its small community of Christian Brothers of my era have all passed on to their reward: Brother George Whelan the Superior; Brother Ephraim Green; Brother Comerford; Brother Arthur; Brother Benignus; Brother Roche; Brother Keegan; Brother Treacy; and Brother White. These names adorn a roll of honour etched gratefully upon the hearts of hundreds of society's outcasts who received shelter, bodily and spiritual sustenance, and education at a critical stage of their lives.

Those gentle, tender, kind men, illustrious disciples of Edmund Ignatius Rice, their order's saintly founder, had, as young men, given up home and family for a celibate life devoted to the care and education of poor children whom society had rejected. In fulfilling his vocation, each man became a substitute father to thousands of fatherless boys, gave his love and his all to 'These, the least of my little ones', sought no earthly reward and got none, save that of seeing their charges grow up God-fearing Christians and good citizens.

Brother Treacy fell seriously ill a year or so after I left school, as though the strain of coming back from retirement to prepare boys for the Post Office exams had been too much for his frail body to bear. I cycled out to see him as soon as I heard, and sat by his bed in his tiny, darkened, cell-like room. Never robust at the best of times, he looked even smaller and frailer. Supported by pillows to ease his breathing, he thanked me for coming to see him. I was ill at ease, at a loss to know what to do or say, never having been in such a situation. In silence I smoothed his pillows, thinking wistfully of the boundless knowledge his head contained. I thought of Goldsmith's immortal phrase: 'and still the wonder grew / that one small head could carry all he knew'. He asked me to promise him I'd look after my job in the Post Office, and keep in touch with my studies to better myself. He pressed the point with great sincerity, looking earnestly into my face as though it meant all the world to hear my promise. I gave it sincerely, with both hands in his, and it pleases me greatly to say that I kept that promise. In a little while I asked if I could fetch anything for him, and if he were in any pain. He said not, and added, 'The only thing I feel is a terrible tiredness. I'm very . . . very . . . tired.' As I placed my hand on his forehead, I urged him to get some sleep, and presently I tiptoed from the room.

'What's your opinion of our patient?' Brother George asked me, one adult to another.

Responding in like manner, I said, 'Oh, I'm sure he'll be all right. He's just very tired, that's all. He told me so. I wouldn't worry about that, no one ever died from tiredness.' But I was wrong. Brother Treacy did, not long after. He had spent himself for us, for me. He was seventy-seven.

No boy left the school without a job, secured for him by the Brothers. There was a steady demand for such boys, especially in country towns and among the farming community, and no wonder. Stories of blatant exploitation filtered back to their friends in school, for schools like Carriglea and Artane were regarded as easy pickings, ready sources of cheap labour. There were many instances of boys working on farms from dawn till sunset for little food and no wages, their employers claiming that their pay was being lodged for them in the Post Office. A boy named John Foy, hired as a tailor by a gents' outfitter and farmer in the midlands for two shillings a week (a shameful wage, even in those days), was more often owed his wages than paid them. His employer – a county councillor, a respected pillar of society – had him milking cows at six o'clock every morning, doing other farm work until the shop opened at nine, working as a tailor until six in the evening, and returning to the farm to work until nightfall.

Gerry Devereux, hired as a tailor in Ballaghadereen, was obliged to work on a farm as well. And his pay for a sixteen-hour day? Less than a shilling a week plus board. He left before me and we corresponded for a time afterwards. I'll never forget a phrase used in a letter of his: 'This must be the coldest shed in all Ireland.' He was warned on the first day that if he ever as much as spoke to one of the farmer's family he'd be sacked on the spot. Even the other labourers kept aloof, and were allowed their meals in the kitchen of the main house. Gerry had to eat his in the outhouse or shed which was now his home. He once described walking between the kitchen and shed with snow blowing into his plate of stew. He slept on straw and occasionally had to sacrifice his covering of sacking to stuff it under the door, to keep out the cold wind. He was maltreated, bullied, abused, poorly fed, and when he suffered a broken leg after being kicked by a cow at milking time, he was summarily dismissed. His sad plight came to the ears of James Dillon, the deputy leader of Fine Gael and TD for the area, who, like the Good Samaritan of old, saw that the boy was looked after in hospital. He must also have arranged payment of compensation for Gerry, because Gerry was able to set up his own tailoring business in Dublin a few years later, which supported him into his old age.

Small wonder that many chucked up their jobs and emigrated to England to join the army, the RAF or the Royal Navy. To these boys they were just other 'institutions' offering food and shelter, plus a regular wage. In time they would be sucked into the maelstrom of the Second World War, from which, sadly, many never returned, breathing their last in foreign fields – at Dunkirk or, like Percy Wynne, in the famous episode commemorated in the film *A Bridge Too Far*. Those whose whitened bones lie at the bottom of the ocean include my poor friend Willie Morrison, whom I admired so much, and who, you will remember, couldn't join the Royal Navy soon enough ('the very minute I leave this place'), and Tripound Cullen, who went down with *HMS Hood*. In many cases there was no telegram sent, no letter written, no 'sad duty to perform' by commanding officer or padre. There was no one to mourn their loss; they were listed under 'No Next of Kin'.

I remember Gerry Devereux, Lord rest him, saying, shortly before he died, that our era was the 'golden decade of Carriglea Park School' and I agreed, wishing I had thought of that. We saw it as a meteor, he said, at its dazzling brightest, before it burned out, after we left. It faded, not because of our going, but because Brother George the Superior was transferred elsewhere and a new dynasty began.

During his tenure of office I was very happy, and I am glad to say I realised it then, although maybe not as much as I do today. I am in the winter of life now and can look back with fondest gratitude to the Brothers. And not without some personal pride too, in having kept my promise to them, which motivated me to progress upwards through eight Civil Service grades before retiring after forty-eight years.

It is important to stress that the shame of my childhood past derived not from my treatment by the nuns or the Brothers, but rather from my treatment at the hands of society at large, in an Ireland which, happily, is no more. Before my story could be related, a new age of enlightenment had first to dawn, bringing a society which places more emphasis on the practice of Christianity than on its outward show; one whose heart is moved to adopt foundlings and 'illegitimates' into hearts and homes; to support widows and poor orphans from state funds and not, with sanctimonious prudery as in the past, to banish children from home and loved ones, rob them of their childhood, and afterwards confine them in limbo.

And glad as I am to have lived to see the new dawn, and

to belong to a new, more enlightened Ireland, so deep go the wounds I sustained on leaving school, and so lasting the shame, that I had intended to take my secret with me, as thousands of others have done. But with that mellowness which old age brings, I have come round to the opinion that it is better to pass my story on, if only to show that there is more to the history of Ireland in the decades after its emergence as a free state than the dry account of her political and economic development that we read in the history books. Now I can publicly acknowledge having been in Carriglea as a child; I can shout from these pages with pride: 'Yes, I was there. I saw Carriglea's "golden decade" and what's more, I am privileged to have belonged.'

On a day in 1938, while cycling in Thomas Street, I saw a small girl being jeered and shouted at by a group of boys. She was returning from school, in the uniform of the Holy Faith convent, and her hair was in two plaits, each ending with a yellow ribbon tied in a bow. I scattered her tormentors, put her schoolbag on the back carrier of my bike and helped her up onto the crossbar. That's what really happened. But as I was seeing it, I wasn't a telegram boy in a uniform with shiny buttons. I was a knight in shining armour, come to rescue a lady in distress and bear her away from danger on my white steed.

She was the nine-year-old daughter of the O'Flanagans of James' Street, whose shop I had recently come to live near. Her parents had taken an instant liking to me on my arrival in the area (they were aware of my background), and the timing could not have been better, for no boy needed friends as much as I did then. A terrible prejudice was abroad towards children (girls as well as boys) from industrial schools. People shouted 'jailbird' and 'bastard' after me in the street. And no wonder, for weren't such places held in the eyes of the public as prisons for young offenders. They had the features of prisons, except that there were no bars. When children absconded, as occasionally some did, the wheels of the law rolled into action. They were hunted down by the police like felons, and brought back in shame. Women in my neighbourhood warned their children against associating with me. The mother of one of the other boy-messengers had recently berated the Inspector of Messengers in the office, wanting to know what the Post Office was coming to by employing boys from industrial schools. She demanded to know why her son should have to work with the likes of them. I was present and didn't know where to hide.

Mr and Mrs O'Flanagan and their family (there were four girls and two boys), opened their hearts to me and made me their very own. I was expected for tea every day; I was included in bookings for Jimmy O'Dea's shows in the Gaiety, and for the odd film show. I slept head to toe with the boys when the family went to a small cottage in Bray for summer holidays. All my free time was spent in their home, and it was a foregone conclusion that one day I would marry into the family. This I did in 1953, when I married Agnes, the girl I had rescued in Thomas Street years before. Sadly, her mother didn't live to see our big day. She had died twelve months previously.

Our budget was tight; there was no money for an exotic honeymoon – a B&B in Galway was as far as it could stretch. However, a telegram four days later summoned us back; my mother had suffered a stroke. She died three days after that, a week to the day after our wedding. Had she lived to see her grandchildren, I know that her immense joy in being with them would have – at least in part – compensated for the grief and anguish she had suffered nearly thirty years before at having to sacrifice her children to a cruel and heartless society.

The first of our five children arrived on the first anniversary of our wedding.